At the Intersection of Everything You Have Ever Loved

Poetry by Gayl Teller

ISBN: 0-931289-02-5
Library of Congress No.: 89-61673

SAN DIEGO POETS PRESS
P.O. Box 8630
La Jolla, CA 92038

ABOUT THE ARTIST:
Jedd Strange is a distinguished muralist. In adition to being well-noted for his paintings, he has received recognition for the originality of his drawings and illustrations which have complemented many book designs.

For Paul, Mike and my parents.

CONTENTS

Acknowledgments

Caesura: "A Picture Horology" (Spring 1985).
Compassion Magazine (Pittenbruach Press): "Lace"(Spring 1988) — First Prize.
The Connecticut Writer: "Passover Caribbe" — Honorable Mention — (1987).
Dog River Review (Trout Creek Press): "Passover Caribbe" (Spring 1988).
Lyrical Fiesta (Fine Arts Press): "Treading Water Together" (1985).
New Voices: "A Hair's Breath" (forthcoming).
Northland Quarterly: "Nostalgic" (forthcoming); "Lace" (1989).
Phoebus: "Hanohano" (Spring-Summer 1985).
Pikestaff Forum: "Menstruation" (forthcoming).
The Reading Series (K-Bar Press): "Patchwork" (Fall 1986).
A Shout in the Street (Queens College Press): "Northern Lights" (1982).
South Coast Poetry Journal: "A December Morning Decision" (Fall 1987).
Suburban Wilderness Press: "Salvation: Recovery Room" (forthcoming anthology).
Swamp Debs Writing Project Selection (Francis Marion College): "Lace" (1988).
Wide Open: "Overlay: On the Spur" (June 1984).
Wyoming, the Hub of the Wheel: "To Fly" and "What Holds" (August 1988).
National Federation of State Poetry Societies (NFSPS): "Handfast" — Honorable Mention (July 1984).
First Prize Peninsula Library Poetry Competition, Lawrence, NY
        (Grace Schulman, judge): "Handfast," "Treading Water Together,"
        "Old Woman's Plot," "A Picture Horology," "The Jogger and the
        Worm," and "The Trimmer" (1984).
Artemis Poetry Contest of Roanoke Writers Workshop: "Handfast" — Honorable Mention (February 1987).
World of Poetry Silver Award: "Overlay: On the Spur" (1986).
At the Intersection of Everything You Have Ever Loved is catalogued in:
        Bern Porter Collection of Contemporary Letters
        Miller Library
        Department of Special Collections
        Colby College
        Waterville, Maine

Handfast

Like the leaf that has lost the forest
at the end of the endless summer,

I am a long way from home, a long way
from that radiance that burned

a circular band of pallor beneath my wedding ring,
long worn, on the weakest finger of my weaker hand.

This is the blanched track of love
expecting too much of itself,

casting a shadow over my entire body.
Did I wear its star-rapt filigree down

with too constant wearing? I never
could take it off, not for 17 years,

not when I was alone with your letters,
constant as pulsars from basic training's separation,

not when I bathed our baby's raw umbilicus and convulsive fevers,
not when I cleared the table, scraping

the meat-encrusted forks from our mouths,
not when there was such heavy silence in the limbs

of our lovemaking, nor knuckle-deep in the manure
in our garden growing salad greens and love-lies-bleeding

in amaranthine memory with drooping spikes,
our curses and caresses grown indistinguishable

in the mulch of our years together,
not even when it was the only thing left

till my nakedness and I loved another man.
At the end of basic training, as new wife,

when you came home passionate and pale —
so much thinner than the husband I had conjured,

I learned the other kind of separation in your returning crush,
the worst loneliness in reunion was separation from a dream.

But now I take off this ring,
now that each bombarding micron of our lives

has worn down its decorative florentine
to this shiny, thin smoothness of itself,

now that each bombarding micron of our lives
has burnished it like an artifact of our ancient hearts,

now that the most durable part remains.
I shiver to be so undressed and disconnected.

What is this pallid border of my life on my hand
that is so smooth, that if I keep my eyes closed,

its presence is as impalpable as the underside of a mindless
wheel that would keep me on its circular course,

making no allowances for traveling conditions,
yet having no hub of its own without my finger?

Do I keep a ghost on my hand,
the ghost of anything that claims to be solidly precious,

or as irrevocable as the heart's commitments once made?
Is this the negative space of memory's resplendent photograph,

or the pale afterimage of a moment's throbbing insight?
Yes, my heart is not a constant meter,

it skips beats, and races away, and slows down to itself,
and is haunted by that guilt.

But now I am only sorry you still believe
in that temple of separation that makes ideal lovers,

but not sinewy mates. And just when I'm sure
everything you would say to me has already been

said or lost, you ask me to tell you definitely
I no longer love you, so we might love again.

Maybe when winter blusters near I will forget
passion's radiance revealed this ghost on my hand,

but will remember the metal tie we ringed
around our avocado tree to support it in its thinness

and how that unnatural metal ring
enabled the tree to outgrow its limited hold

and became so enmeshed in its most vital tissue
that we couldn't remove that ring

without ripping apart some very essence of that tree.

Treading Water Together

He curves his lean stroking
        way toward me, puffs a cloud
breath, a visible warmth

made clearer by cold. His fears
        are warm because he says them
to me, inside shapes of fog.

It's surprisingly easy to speak
        in private water like this, no
crowd of other demands, for once.

Why don't we do this more often?
        Remember this spot. We'll pretend
we've made our mark crossing mud-

bottomed, slippery shallows,
        the jagged way of rocks and
chipping out secrets between

which twist, which ruin, pretend
        we could foresee looking back
down this channel's silt, find

this emotion's greening imbroglio
        toward the swift currents sweeping us
together, pretend we leave tracks

in water, but who could
        inhabit the quicksand of memory
foretold? Not even now while

his familiar invisible call
        strays out more whole in hazy words
wafting softness onto his crisp

open-and-shut eye just floating on
        deep green, not even as a spectrum flits
between us, iridescently, then

invisibly in our plunging grasp.
        We kiss. What's vulnerability got
to do with love? Underbreath, under-

water, I look up at his look rippling
        in clouds. I've been afraid a long time
I'd drown to know him so.

Splash.

A Picture Horology

[F o r   m y   s o n]

Having no need
but to be torn and torn
anew from sheet after sheet of self,

from the eidetic European bridge whose arches

never complete themselves but go on forever down
in photographed stone, or in what we believe

is something strong and supportive
as stone uprights under the family on the bridge,
disappearing down in the bottomless water, the calendar

that hangs by a thread in his room, like its water,

has no picture all its own
but takes on and lets go whatever looks into it.

And that is how the gurus tell you to get out of bed
to a new morning, to tear away the sheets
to whatever picture you never quite suspected,

for man tells time by pictures.

It takes on and lets go whatever his magic
marker red-circles around its blind square eyes,

whatever raw blue skies get cut with red clay
rooftops and cobblestone roads where he's never been
that enter and admit the shape of his indelible wind

as he drums his snare, there in his music's growing

tangle of the everywhere of the not-here
and throbs with the calendar's distance in his eyes.

It was too soon to be torn
from my warm sheets,
but early that morning he untucked me

and yanked off the one with the solid red tulips

to his all new tableau vivant I couldn't believe
was he standing there in a dim glimmering light

cut with his elegance in a charcoal tuxedo, flaming
red cummerbund, sharp patent leather shoes, glossy as water
around his feet, and the piercing edge

of unexpected perception. There,the familiar archway

still delicately suspended over his darkling eyes. There
the hieratic stance of lost boyhood, the classic posture

that splintered in the waters gathering
in the breathless moment
my eyes dared fully yield

at his admission.

And if I had the strength I would have run
for the camera, or for something, but

as usual there would have been no preparation made,
no film to condense from that auroral glimmering
what was not visible, and never would be again —

but in split-seconds, as when he grabbed my hand

forgetting his guard, on the curdling brink
of his seat in a movie house,

and I felt each stripling finger gently
withdraw itself to its own
hand that was the shadow clock of mine

to indicate it was time, was time.

What Is This Pull-Over?

[F r o m   m y   s o n]

What's wrinkled with detaching warmth —
warmth yet brooding in the tucked plush
fabric from the heart of fresh muffins,
and mittens just flipped to the floor
with a careless suspender draggling,
chinkity-chankity across a kitchen
that is no longer there, with a window
to the snowman in the yard, his beet eyes
bleeding backwards through his head the way
my blood seeps through the frozen image?

"Would you wear it, ma?" he smirked.

What's hanging loosely about my breasts
to be tucked in to some shadowy place —
place that keeps sliding on breath's
rising, falling, crescendo, descrescendo,
the edging popping out around him,
a flapping from that sense of being, a soloist,
and we rose applauding in the auditorium,
the burgundy seams still bound tight,
precluding how winter light would window
through each pore in the thready binding
of this passed-on pull-over from my son
to dazzle and chill to my bone?

What Holds

[T o B. F., a n a s t r o p h y s i c i s t]

[I]
it all together? Searching, we toy around with more
solidities, you with your clusters of black holes
with white hole undersides, sucking in our mind-spangled
universe, and I with my new part-time job and latest poem
to secure my galactic moorings.

We make our languages rich with vice versas — like fission
and fusion, you and I make we. We spin the universe
into our private palindrome in which to play. Still we're left
wondering what our little quirks and quarks are made of,
each answer begetting the next question — a kind of infinity
in either direction, like searching through the mutual mirrors
of our fears.

Sometimes I can get so squeezed down into my regrets,
so crushed by it all, hope, even laughter emerges
in little expansive waves across my abdomen as if
I were pregnant again, swells pushing from where
nothing seemed to matter, vibrating out into the air
to fluster the universe.

How can what's burnt out consume more than what burns?
How can a black hole in the heart be our densest matter?
So you insufflate the white hole of creation, and I release
the electric keys to a new horizon. Is it just our nature
to believe the blackest glower there is, our densest matter,
turns outward to being, not just another compelling hole,
that to go to pieces is always to heal?

[II]
When opening a new box of crackerjacks, as a child,
I would keep feeling around for the little picture
with those clear, superimposed lines that could shift
everything split-seconds around into a new one,
then get fuzzy again.

But lately, more and more, I have been wondering what keeps
my wandering luminants spinning within their shivering
shells of meaning within the dark of me. There was no Big Bang.
God just dissolved with his talons and fangs and mercilessness
at 17 when I declaimed I hated him — ducked down just in case —
"You need a shrink! Nothing that strong, that great needs
to be praised so much!"

By the time I thought I clearly understood no matter
how concrete, how dense, it's not an image that generates
the universe that is the love that is the poem,
whether scanned like a chalk cosmos on a blackboard
by school children, tagged with the creator's glorious name,
or pulled to smithereens in my black-ribboned hands,
I revised the search again, for if I had center,
I wouldn't need to be praised, and without center,
praise would be too fickle.

In this my 38th year of the search, riffling through
printout pages wielding students' fragile lives
for the crystallized details that cohere, I think
of all the people who have riffled through my life and just
moved on. Where is the girl who pricked her finger with mine
and swore she'd always be my blood sister?

I tagged torrid lovers and commitment to paprika/soap-flake
routines, to miscellaneous poems, to the husband of my childhood,
the man of my son, as we move ever further away from where
we were, or is it ever further toward? and I have returned
to the mulberry garden, basting my toes in its indelible wine,
and as this hemisphere tilts away from its flaming source,
I am drawn more by the shrinking mass of crimson asters
as if each fermenting, falling petal were some former
amputation of the heart of things.

Is everything a matter of perspective the way the light can be
solidity or wave depending on what you ask of it and it of you?
Is love that cherished face or some force of illumination
within?

After having tagged holes as solids and solids as holes,
I in my way as you in yours, should we ever dare to admit
it's in no object, in nothing with mass, in nothing out there
holus bolus central enough, are we then just impelled further along
and further and further toward that strong strong force of undoing?

A Million Million Minute Mouths

Sucking on the undersides of the canary orange
leaves of my favorite croton, my god! what
spider mites, a million million minute mouths
mutilating what I love, the crisscrossings
of their sly spun networks best seen
when the light dazzles most — like this —
setting the canary color into aureolin song.
Sometimes just this shimmering alone is enough,
or it's the shaft to longing, or a poem.
This morning I spray a legion of breathing legs still
and feel less guilt than if I killed just one.
Their eggs, ad infinitum, white ammo pellets,
await their signals for firing.

Then I flea powder my Twinkle, my cat —
"Nothing kills the eggs," the vet tittered.
"You can soak 'em in alcohol or gasoline,
but control's all you can hope for, I fear.
You can't get rid of those darn little pests
even if you lock-up your Twinkle inside" —
Poor Twinkle — each pest generates generations
whose existential end is to pierce his skin,
suck his blood, bite him, bite him, suck,
get in his eyes, every second, of his every inch,
of his every day. I brush a sordid snow
of eggs and feces, larvae and fleas, falling
from his scabbed belly — *Behold the hand of the Eternal*
will be against the cattle that is in the field,
against the horses, the donkeys, the camels,
the oxen and the sheep, and against my Twinkle,
a very grievous plague is humming in my head,
haggadah *boils, vermin, locusts, disease, darkness* —
Raid, flea powder siftings my matinal incense.

Sucking on the undersides of my backyard serenaders —
while I with paper and seeds refill my feeder
and Twinkle goes off to prance and prey —
while we are all stranded together in the sun —
pincered lice with their parasites to the Nth degree
in every red cardinal, blackbird and chicadee,
in every blue jay, sparrow and mourning dove.
Every songbelly has been bloodied, and every poem
has a bloody mouth. *Behold*, parasite on parasite
sucking on fear, biting on joy, I can feel
so drained sitting here with my pencil points.

Every squirrel that feeds my spirits at my sill
is swill to a million hungers he feeds live,
hornworms are chewing up my tomatoes on the vine
while wasp larvae are eating through the hornworms,
because to be alive is to be consumed right through
their loud, rich chevrons, to their little regal horns.
And there's a parasite especially fitted to each host
when most vitally alive, sucking on the undersides
of every good feeling I have. *Behold*, the sucker
of the Eternal — self-doubting leech that can
attach itself to hope's most cockeyed membrane,
sapping its sweetness nearly, not completely, dry,
because it's the living doubt lets hope thrive.

Menstruation

[H a n u k a   S c e n a r i o]

The kitchen witch cants on the shelf
as I stir up the bubbling cauldron
of canadles netted in tradition's dill,
diced parsnips and butcher-blocked chicken.

The thin tin cover is rapping
as if the brewing heart beneath could speak.
Strangely, what will nourish begins with sting
as out of onion vapors teardrops streak,

as my oily fingers streak ire across the glitter
wrappings of all these gifts I enlisted to get.
I grate a nail tip or two, a raw knuckle blister
into the latke batter, thus humanize it,

and curse at the vapors as they rise
to the heavens from my home,
seeping from the machine spinning my things dry
that I'd rather be writing a poem,

when what to my wine-shot eyes should appear
but my husband whistling his way, dropping popcorn
crumbs into my cuisinart, sour apple tart, mise en scene —
Cut! my director calls. *Where is it written*

you blunder your way through a battlefield
of a holiday lit like a fairy tale with religious fires
and its ogres simmering in your blood like a Maccabean Macbeth
as if all the tragic vapors of humankind conspire —

take your sister-in-law sobbing she's not coming
to the party to sit at the same table
with her husband, they have spent their morning
flinging flapjacks like grenades, imprecating all trouble,

gut or heart, the worse the better, for each other:
take their 4-year-old smacking everyone in the same spirit:
take your sister not·abiding the whacking tongue of your mother
that bucks on its fears like á broomstick

to your father: take your father-in-law's silence
as self-appointed general of squabble
months at a time lunging at his wife
with his sword of wordlessness all spit-shined and able:

take your husband spoiling your son, your baby,
by labelling him spoiled: then take
your son craving more labels, buying his ID
shirt after ID shirt, a toady to every penny raked —

to your hate? to your hurt? to your anger?
Where is it written? In what script?
my director intones. *And before your upstage action,*
take one stone thrown by a youth shot in the Gaza strip,

take one finger blown off a vendor in Ireland,
take one breast hacked off a pollster in Haiti,
take one rat belly bloated with human blood
in a Guatamalan prison, take one abscess from the brain

of a detainee drugged 6 years in a Soviet mental ward,
take one hair from the head of a child chained
in a closet, take one pubic hair from the veteran's
testes electrified in Vietnam, take any mote of mayhem,

stir deep into your own rattling cauldron,
soup of boiling, soup of blood,
soup of stinging, soup of tears. Brew long.
Brew well. Rekindle as human food.

"What smells so sweet?" my husband asks, as I press
"play" for the new tape my son synthesized for me
and offer them latkes, as Kermit the Frog purls, "someday
we'll find it, the rainbow connection," through soup steam.

Cut! That's a wrap for now — my director beams.

Still Life

Afternoon alone, off traipsing
through common chickweeds with an abstract
half-poem and my resolution to be
neither wife nor mother again —

at least not till clock hands clasped each other
at midnight's lone stroke
and anger's thin ichor thickened
to a less godly-clear blood —

I found Safety Town, where kids are taught
the rules of the road, unlocked, so I went in.
Everything was smaller, like suddenly
looking at your life through binoculars

backwards. Each vacant little house was composed
of one impossible room, about head-high
and schoolday-groomed in fast-drying,
solid storybook tones.

Through prefabbed cardboard walls
windows pierced the inner dark to needless intricacy.
You could see right through
to the blazing blankness of garden paths.

No frail lace yellowed
with memories breathed there,
nor any other such domestic subtleties,
for this was a town that taught movement,

not residence. Computer-perfect,
a model of compressed directionals
for how to go
up and down nameless streets,

plotted, dotted, and arrowed, even broken-up
for the sake of learning to cope.
Tots strapped to wheels
would whizz into ripeness

on roads gala as Christmas
with red and green balls of light
on a central timer strung
by sophisticated nomads. Ah, it was good

to get away where miles unfolded
in blocks without time or place or human voice,
drawn on and on by the mercurial
appeal of the intersection in remoteness.

All primed for movement, nothing moved
in this deserted still life I somehow entered
like the quiet eye of a storm
with my common love

of distance that had brought me here,
a joy I get peering through
the other end of the eyepiece
every now and then.

Hanohano

Diamond Head

We wake in our night
and it is day. All streets
sound the same. Our language
is squeezed into a few letters
that somehow can say it all. All
disorientation is purposeful
pilgrimage, hopefully, as
on this eroded trail
underfoot and on the tongue
of the native guide who speaks
pidgin to the tourists and
English to the other guide.
Cliffteasers, gaspers, lovers
of elevation with guardrails,
we'll clamber all that way up,
up, along the uncertain edge,
from lookout to lookout to
look down, eventually, into the
oracular gape of lunar earthscape.
We mount a tower of sooted
stairs; ahead, they disappear
into a dark, forbidding tunnel
like menehunes who do their
most work in least visibility.
When they emerge high as air
on a thin, scintillant
ribbon of trail, some begin
snapping my picture with
the stranger akin to me as we
follow in their footsteps' ascent
to otherworldly vision.
He is from some tinroof town
on no tour stop, a laborer,
pineapple picker, cane burner,
who knows; and I some tourist
with my own automatic eye.
But now, far enough away,
we are hanohano, glorious
and exalted by distance;
married into their family albums,
we will be passed down together.

From the House of the Sun

[H a l e a k a l a]

Here on the ash altar
of desolation   arid lava flows
her firepit's multihues   across the arcane
cinder cones   across her mute-lipped
old spatter vent   across the fire goddess Pele's
awesome black powder and pumice expanse we cross
in our cramped surface ways   Here the demigod Maui
lassoed the fireball in its abstruse track   as gift
he gave his mother dear to dry her tapa cloth Above treeline
upon undifferentiated cloudscape   our shadows greatly magnified
and colored   we are our own specters   we the otherworldly guests
in the house of the sun   Here untrammeled silence is our best medium
We hear bubbles of ascent   burst in our ears   with unspeakable
clarity   all too fast   reclaimed   by the peregrine mists
that haunt such heights   Here we come so close   to what is barren
we tremble   through the fiery pits   of our own eruptive emotion
We almost acquiesce   to whatever is   so indigenous to dry cinder
terrain that waits   with silversword dagger-leaves   20 years or more
to flower   just once   the generic height of a man   to die
We almost acquiesce   to whatever is   so unsettling so exotic
in emptiness   we must hold ourselves back   on the rim
of new vantage point   where we look out on our own   feral and multihued
love of what we fear   "Being on the inside looking out is the best way
to see the crater"   we have been told by a ranger that twirls a toy troll
In the presence of absence   his voice becomes icon-solid   sculptured
by the quiet   so that it is hard to resist his admonition   so har to
resist the curse locked in volcanic debris   so that we would be cursed
forever and ever for spiriting off   just one piece of the house of the sun

The Trimmer

[For a kamaaina]

It smokes, it heaves, it erupts —
it is the land. A starkness
and a fiery red dream's debris
stretching up broad-leaved
trees heavy with milk and sweet,
succulent meat; fat mangoes on tall
shades; the oval ripening passion
fruit of the vine; purple tough-skinned
avocado bellies; a flamingo extravagance
in poinseanna panache; colas as thick
as children's paint brushes, dripping
with resin; bananas swelling upside-down
like fetuses; the diurnal haue
dawning pale flowered, dropping
bloodshot at sunset.

It is the land, that is always
happening to her and through her,
a smoking, heaving, erupting
into sensibility as she goes
toward her life, with an unborn
life, always being just beyond
her own grasp, like a bird
of paradise poised for flight,
rooted into the iron soil.

From high on misty cliffs
where rainwater catches in crevices
of the domed terrain, then plunges
great distances into deepening pools,
she has meandered in her pursuits
of the outgoing-inflowing sea
that gathers, surges, breathes
and weaves its tracery with weeds
and thought, with blowhole blasts
through lava tubes.

Inside her earplugs, around
the unmoving ear stones, she hears
the land. It is never silenced
under her plastic-bagged hair.
It hums as through seashell chambers.
It fills spaces between the cold,
hollowed cylinders of sun she takes,
tilts, trims, tosses, takes,
tilts, trims, tosses back to
the continuous flow of decrowned
pineapple parts from between her
plastic-bagged fingers, wielding
a steel blade against the sweet grain
of the land, inside a row of inexorable
rows of trimmers, packers, noise-leveled
tongues, sliced, chunked, crushed.
It is the land inside a centrifuge
of sweetness, the flavor spinners,
the grey towers of stacked cans
glued to sunshine with labels
to all tongues of the world
that crave the sweet taste of the land.

"You got stink ear?" an aikane asks
her under the giant steel pineapple
rising 195 feet, as the night shift ends
and she leaves with the dented ones,
the haue about to bloom, wanting sleep,
to sleep the menehune sleep of stone.

kamaaina — longtime island resident
to get stink ear — to not listen
aikane — friend
menehunes — a mythical gnome-like race that worked only at night
    hauling huge rocks. According to legend, if a menehune
    labored too long and got caught by the sun, he was
    turned to stone.

To Fly

[I]   Flight of a Ground Bird

DON'T TAP ON THE GLASS

I had been watching a hornbill, a hefty bird,
not particularly colorful with dull grey
indigo feathers, a feeder of the ground
that kept the taste of its grit as he bore
his casque of solid ivory (carved up
for centuries as an Eastern art) into flight.
As far-sighted and high-hearted as any bird,
he lofted into a flightspan that stunned:
each time the clear cage was struck,
the bird from the Old World faltered down
to a leafless perch on a disembowered stump,

. . . but made his broad spring, top-heavy
    . . . lift-off, and dipped his wing
       . . . in air again as over sunny,
       . . . acacia scrub, breathing in flight,
. . . breathing out flight, dipping his wing,
    . . . and in that routine looping he was,
       . . . a zookeeper would tell you,
       . . . free, when he didn't try to fly
. . . through that fixed window that flashed
    . . . him back his own flapping, his own
       . . . bucking, what vitreous humor,
       . . . to see the inlay of transparency
. . . was his own strange feathers in his eyes!

and got smacked to his stump again. Thrown
by his own force, a zookeeper would tell you
that the bird creates the cage anew each time
he tries to fly through. Cloven from streaming
clouds, would he ever learn to stop charging
the invisible cage and live quietly within
its gimlet-eyed discipline? Would stiffness
seep into his wing as into the docile
more learned birds of long encagement?

With the earth in his mouth, in his blood,
the sky that wasn't there was calling him,
a creature believed to mate for life, locked
in solitary, shrieking out, a jarring call —
true to its source in grittiness, for wasn't
all birdsong wafted from tension in the throat
that the song only partly releases, a trembling
fleshy limpness hanging on it. What good now
that broad wingspan without access to vastness?

[II]   Flight of an Underground Bird

Toward some far-sighted air, some distant zenith
that might not even be there, like a burning star
to a caged bird that's just a haloed bulb
in an electric socket past some dark hallway,
yet he wrote his compassion, not to hope,
but to breathe, to hear, *to hear the voices
in the earth and to lose yourself in memory of sky
when the morning is fresh. When you have forgotten
about the aches of night. To fly . . .*

And in his flight shadowed by security police,
arrested, condemned to polishing stone floors
till they mirrored his mind — often his only
contact with light where phantasms shifted
moment to moment like the interrogator's face
that turned out to be his own, being alone,
and seeing alone, and needing alone, alone
in the dark, with *the dark mirror brother:*

in maximum security for the terror of his humanism,
his poetry pinioned to the underground, his voice
learning the rasp of silence, he made his broad spring
and dipped his words on a cache of snippets —
*denying the humanity of the person facing you
is a sure-fire way of diminishing* — and got locked
in the *bomb* again, and deprived of food
and any extra words they snipped off letters
from loved ones that exceeded the limit,
while the Majorkeeper watched him for symptoms
of his anti-apartheid vision, flew into
a rage if the prisoner showed any of the signs
of behaving like a *mister* instead of a *bandiet* . .

That night, reading about Breytenbach's imprisonment,
I thought about the hornbill's battered casque,
how like a palimpsest inscrutably scrawled
with the Old World, it was a testament to some
ancient urgency to erect enclosures for flight,
to be the keeper of the unpartakable wing,
to come and watch how it falters within
its shrunken empyrean, as it tries to loft itself
up off the ground into the spiritless uplift
of the stagnant air, and how in that cage,
like at the invisible edge of understanding
where every window becomes a mirror, suddenly,
I saw my own face reflected, reflected both ways.

*Quotations from *The True Confessions of an Albino Terrorist*

Anhedonia on the Brink

In a cage, amidst a bounty of apples
    and grapes, they perched at the hollow

of a truncated tree where a suggestion of a nest
    pouted. Emptied now. During breeding season,

the female plastered herself inside the tree,
    leaving only a slit wide enough for the tip

of her beak to receive food from her mate
    as often as 40 times an hour for about 100 days,

inside the walls of instinct without light or flight.
    Today I watched the pair of hornbills couple in haggling

over one seedless grape, deadlocked in the foretip
    of the female cageling's at least foot-long beak.

She would not capitulate to the bite of hanker
    her mate harassed her with deep under the feathers

of her inwardly drawn, unaloft wing,
    which it seemed he would release only on the condition

that she surrender that very meager grape, on the brink
    of consummation, from her megabeak into his megabeak.

Nor, it seemed, could she penetrate that iota
    of pleasure for fear of losing it in the toss

toward her craw down that long stretch
    of prolonged mouth where she was vulnerable.

To thwart his "checkmate," she thrust her grape-laden bill
    like a loaded BB gun into the hole of the defoliated tree

where she had instinctively shut him out before
    with her own droppings and the mud he brought her.

Nest now was bunker where she could keep
    her minute fruit, like a weapon or trophy in the hollow

darkness, so long as she didn't try to enjoy it.
       And he, in utter frustration, bit harder into her wing

for what she wouldn't release in utter
       giving for him to nibble from her nib

and what apparently wouldn't taste the same
       from the floor's largesse in their cage as that snatched

victoriously from her beak. When she couldn't endure
       his crass bites any more, she unsheathed the point

of her beak from the tree, with verdant trove
       nakedly revealed. But without her ceding

that globule of juice, he was not satisfied
       and sharply snapped at her encumbered beak,

rendered a hundred times heavier by that one
       little grape, until she plunged beaklong

into the bole hole again, and he resumed
       his style of coupling with his keenest edge

into her wing. They seemed truly
       stalemated in their enclosed eden.

I wondered how they kept from starving
       in the midst of plenty. Maybe yesterday

he had been It with the grape in his beak
       and her beak grounded his wing. I pictured

each feeding alone in dark corners
       when the other wasn't looking.

       A couple I knew had lots of headgear too
with all sorts of laminated degrees

       displayed in their master bedroom over shelved
ivory sculptures of miniature towns he got

       in the war. He was a chemical engineer
and an embodiment of chemistry, his face

often flushed at parties and praise
for his original tiffany shades.

She was a corporate attorney, quick-on-the-draw
with words, her anecdotal canapes always a hit.

But she kept her whimsical wax
sculptures hidden inside a buffet

to do her shaping in the middle of the night.
They too dined alone,

she said because they lived different hours,
he was on when she was off, and vice versa.

It wasn't just how he teased her
at their party that he couldn't savor

his food with her watching, she was too
hard-up for compliments, too disgusted

by his lip contortions, he said. But after
the tour through their mirrored

wine cellar where he filled our crystal goblets,
and after we toasted at their picture

window overlooking their greenhouse in their magnificent
Greenwich colonial — whose gourmet termites

one day she hoped to afford to feed, she said,
and clinked to his latest tiffany

shade overhead, and after we ooed and aaaed —
each facet of colored glass so precisely a polished

cut of his light iridescently held
in joints of melted lead —

it was how she confessed for him, that
pieces were coming down and the shades

weren't selling, and it was how he kissed her
for the good news she hadn't shared with him,

and how he didn't know why he had to find out
from Terry Zell that one of her wax creatures

won third prize at the craft fair. It was *Ignis Fatuus,*
the one he had called *Boogie Man,*

she said, the one he said she should light
at dinner at the party . . .

When the male cageling flew off
to other purposes at another end of the cage,

what he had abandoned as sour
hardly seemed any sweeter to her

as she persisted in hiding her treasure,
that sudden splash of center unreleased

from the minute outline of fullness,
the bite somehow even more insidious

in the biter's absence.

Perspectives in Green

[Bronx Botanical Gardens]

The lighter green called spring
in a child's crayon box
is the moss underneath the head
of a damp-soaked man, leaning
on an embrasure crook of the earth,
his body pulled in close to itself
on discarded newspaper, passive
to the accumulation of rain:

and the glass compress cool as dreamlight
he keeps upon his thirsty lips
of the pintsize bottle he drinks from —
a kind of reassuring bud
revealing its warmer undertones
and a returning blur of fullness
as he nudges the bottle neck
half-through the opened earth-
brown paper pod — inscribed *Ed's Discounts:*

and the underside of his wheeze as he hums,
saturated with something barely audible
to the three arm-linked girls, sashaying by,
drowned out again in the maelstrom of mating frogs,
shrilling carriage wheels, sense-chafing gusts.

Every so often he says something to anybody.
Whatever is missing or hasn't been found
collects around his talk to a self-contained
silent space between the certain winds.
They purge his spattered words
as quicklime would whitewash graffiti
from a noble park monument,
an anonymous note bleeding through.

His eyes, thick-crusted around the rims, spill
over from some trapped source, some feverish fluid
that can't fully escape and run its course,
nor dry up and be finished — inexorable hot waterfall
the cool wind can't possibly absorb.
He doesn't bother to wipe off what dissolves
the greening charioteer on its pedestal
into incomprehensible shimmer on a wobbling shadow.

The spring air is heavy to tow — Spat! —
just a burden of sweet scents to lose
through the moss in his lungs.
"If I tell you to walk fast, then walk faster,"
a woman admonishes a child, pulling him closer,
away from that grubby, misplaced man whose eyes
are helpless enough to dangerously confront
her own helplessness in the fenced-in field
of what she can explain in the herb garden
to the boy, bearded in custard, looking baffled
back at the man with the pitted face,
his ear to an earth bed, who reached up —
he saw the man reach up to give him something —
with his gnarled fingers bleeding soil —
"Is he going to sleep or listening for something?"

The man rolls over to his other side, relieved
of having to go elsewhere. His back is exposed
to a semblance of himself the soft ground keeps
like some vague memory, a dream looming as the boy
in the herb garden in an ancient howling,
who is compelled to get up high, on tiptoe
on a wobbly bench to see the man on the ground.
"Didn't we know that man in our old house?"

Climbing the shadow to get into the shimmer,
the boy is as lambent to the man as the shimmer
to the boy footing the bronze horse. Each reaches
for it because it can't be held. The boy is
that restless transparency balancing over the man
who touches what custard clots his beard.

Muscle ties come loose, he smiles for no one.
Something else is wobbling loose like the heaviness
of a statue melting away. Somewhere deeper relief
is distilled without the mess of human hands.

While the furry fists of moss thrust another spring-
green up through the mud where he roots down
his fingers to the arcane magnet of the earth
and the electric-yellow forsythias come charging
out through their wood, a vaguely familiar boy
comes running from the shimmering herb garden,
"What did you want to give me, Mister?"

[37]

The Intersection of Two Women

Her groceries are light as hollow bones —
she carries her daughter's
one demand-fed meal, once a worknight —
one bile-skinned pear
one pus-blooded banana
one head unraveling lettuce.
It's all the swamp of green
mucous succotash around and
around inside the torn paper sack
she supports in interlinked fingers,
feels an inner rolling of her own.

She still dresses up the Park Ave. woman
she was before Benjamin died:
full velvet suit, 14k gold choker.
They say she gave away caviar at Halloween,
scooped it right into the kids' bags.
Her posture, her coiffure, still impeccable,
each black-laden lash waterproofed
so at work, no one really knows.

Camouflaged in color and scented pride,
she always takes too large a bag
each and every twilight
to deliver fresh her daughter's
green non-caloric things
after each and every talking day,
careful to say nothing
at the telephone switchboard tentacles:
a ritual by ghostlight,
by crosstown busfumes, by portalbell,
by third eye at the peephole.
Almost pure soul now rendered
from the defatted skeletal frame
left of her womanchild, behind the bolted
interface, who holds up the little circle
in her blade hand, controls the vision
through the one-way glass eye,
observes the black order of hollows
in her mother's hair, counts the fruit
as her mother kneels to position them
under the shut steel orifice.
"Amy, I know you're there!"

The older woman props herself
to eye-level with the other,
to the double-woman-backed-looking-glass
distortion that takes them both
into its circle, and divides them.
She sees her own made-up eye reflected wrong.
"Amy, can I see you today? Amy?"
The other woman observes the fringe,
spider legs over her mother's eye.

"I only brought what you wanted. I promise,
no candy...Amy? I know you were in
my apartment. It was you, wasn't it, Amy?
The sheet on the couch, the door left open —"
The blackout lid gets lowered in stages:
first the hair goes, then the eyes,
then the ears and nose, then the mouth.
"I told that janitor off! 'Wasn't my daughter,'
I said, 'who smashed eggs on the incinerator.'
Amy? Amy, I found a new doctor. Amy?
Why are you — to me, I mean — all you have
to do — just eat. Get better because —"
Her mother is totally featureless now
under the lowering steel edge
of the fixed eye on the closed door.
The lid is dropped again —
the headless woman departs
in steps no longer hushed nor even...

"Oh Niome, you used to be Ben's beauty."
The guillotine is screwed into the glass eye.
In every circumspect step Amy withdraws
in a thousand minute efforts, as if
on stilts in middle age, as if every
unit of step involved making a complex plan
to avoid another fracture, like those
of her hip and ankle after San Francisco,
when she almost split completely away
from here, almost made it wholeheartedly
as five years tanned away in old letters
Niome ribboned around Amy's paste-up
picture life on tennis courts with greased men —
This is it, Ni, the court where we won
the championship! That's Ron.

[39]

Relinquishing her programming of computers,
she's programmed her own weight loss
of a whole woman: free, pure hungerlessness
and bric-a-brac bones. Breastless,
she waits without a germ of craving
for what's in Niome's bag, at the spyglass
window over Central Park, where anorexic leaves
bleed high off and unfallen to the ground,
and lightlessness has already begun
its dissolution of the intersection her mother
crosses with the fluorescent funhouse faces.
How effortlessly it sweeps up the fake blood
and the oversated trick-or-treaters sugared
in delights. Clowns and werewolves devour
what they can get a sequined princess to whore
of her candy for a joy ride in a supermarket cart.
Three Mickey Mice attend Satan's fiery cape —
he pitchforks them off the curb's end —

Niome distributes her pennies among cherubs
and demons alike. Her arms are empty.
She's delivered this night's bag of her child.
Amy waits to be left alone till 9pm's
call through the phonecord for tomorrow's food
order Niome better bring fresh, she told her,
or she won't eat at all, "not a bite, Niome."

Almost far enough away to make contact now,
each waits for the other's eyes, the flicker
across the abysmal street synapse.
Each mouths a message, through blind slats,
long distance to the other, each tries
to hear the shadows unshaping themselves
on the other's lips. "I love you, Amy."
"If you commit me, Ni, if they force-feed me,
I'll bequeath you my suicide to live with."

Fathoms down there is a constant
ringing now surfacing now blooming
invisibly upon the body fountain,
there's an echoing down hollow spines
of books unending, rereading one faithful
old friend in a letter, regrouping accents
with a phone throbbing facelessness, a bonging
clangorous TV clock blocks each entrance
of silence, and the imperious gabbling

of nothingness begins again, no effort knows
true absence, there's an invisible companion's
all-embracing whistle, reverberating white noise
of all pure sounds, a whole cosmos funneling
her fathoms forever down...

                 ...and surfacing
she scrubs salt into the green skin,
props her heart's cage against the ice
cold sink. Her fingers, always cold,
are momentarily warmed in her armpits.
She sniffs the pear, scours the peel
apart — her hard rippling ribs struggle
apart with breath. The thin cells hold on
as the dresses she outshrunk hold on
to her mirrors. Loosening them is hard work.
She sucks cautiously on the insipid edge
of the barest pear jelly, looks at the spotless
stack of scrubbed tuna cans she didn't eat
for Niome. The reluctant tongue touches it,
encircles it like an alien, pushes it
back out the lips. She sucks it back in,
perspiring, and swallows the insipid thing.

At the pear's end, at the hour's end,
the woken life snarls colicky revenge
at the intruder within. Her heart,
draining itself from each cryptic corner
of desire, beats itself hard.
She unbags the loose head — insipid iceberg —
she must eat, she must eat,
in this ringing skull or be bagged
in a hospital bed. She must eat,
she must eat the whole head, veins and all —
"Niome, you bastard, you couldn't let go!"
Concealed among the leaves, white bread
paste. "Ghost trap. I won't, I won't
materialize for you, Niome!" — contractions
begin in green acid waves spurting out
in convulsive stings — the telephone rings,
the telephone rings, the telephone rings.

Lace

Where the overarching oak was frail
  lace shadow in intimacy
    with our own, we sat,
      my mother and I,

idly watching the wind break patterns
  that would not sit still
    with us, any more than
      we could sit there

in the house full of well-wishing
  strangers after the funeral.
    If not for the gaps,
      the lace before us

would have had no loveliness. On the ground
  we tended so introspectively,
    the negative spaces
      held sunlight

the way you can love a person right through
  his shortcomings. She fed me
    wild berries plucked
      from the shadows,

and like the child that I wasn't, I trusted
  she knew which were poisonous.
    We partook of the sweetblack
      fruit of the tanglevine

together, and on impulse, I thanked her
  for my love of nature. She had died
    so many times in her life,
      her heart understood

the pre-fall tremblings of the tiger lily
  anthers at their peak of pollen.
    With a straight-pin, she kept
      the black lace to her head.

Arboreal

They sent me a homemade map, under my married
name, smudged with secretions from the trails
of their touch — the lymph-spilled scent,
the broken-arrow beckon, were for me to follow
through illegible streets and arteries —

Last time it was my mother's cry
from the end of her broken passageway
to her sister Ruth that their mother was lonely
in her grave, no man next to her to twine into,
their father buried anonymously, somehill, somewhere.
Go visit Mama, Ruth. She's still your mother.
And Ruth, her throat closing in what unhealed
memories kept of the flesh of their father's face
embedded with their mother's broken dream-sockets,
refused to give love to the underyears.
No stone offering would she dig for the dead
love that never freed her to live,
no stone would she place beside the six
small stones bestowed on their mother's tomb —
one for each child gripped and squeezed,
tight as a stone to pass, one for each
rip-out from her body, from her home —
at the site where love is measured in hard units
of starbits, no perpetual care, no ivy guilt-
breaker would she plant for the undermoaning wind.

Last time it was my mother's cry,
her arm twisting in on herself
like a branch out of palpable shadow,
her hair churning in the wind,
her eyes wobbling in their cribs —
Will you visit me?

What I see as far away from me — out there —
O illusion of motion, moves with me
along the nebulous thruway to the ingrained
and knotted cedar house of my cousins.
I breathe in the spirits from the secret seams
in panelled walls, from what clings to the soles
of my shoes, and alleyways cleaved into my hand.
It is all around me, a raw scent, it is
all between us as we kiss, two by two,
on the threshold to the outcrying woods.

Once every year or so I think I know them,
these ravenous familial strangers,
a three-generation congregation around chopped liver
choking up clanmarrow and unmetabolized tidbits,
as we sit around a stone fireplace. The mesh
screen screams apart for our private sharing
the singed yet-yearning tongues of flame.

Rachelle stutters over her husband Alan's name
and lurches it everywhichway in explaining why
she must leave him every night to sleep this year
at her mother's, where air flows out unboxed
by the cinder blocks that lock the walls
of the rooms she and Alan moved to, to have more room
to have a child, at her mother's where the alleyways
are uncongested with the eyes she bade the super
to chase away in the drafty cellar with her
armful of diapers. Her story gushes
with salivary storm, and subsides with telling,
till it needs to be told and retold again.

Alan tries to explain to himself out loud to Aunt Ruth
what Rachelle's therapist said she really said.
Ruth beckons over her husband Ernie, who's been there
when she couldn't explain why she needed more
than there was. Cousin Gloria suggests Alan take Rach
to her Recovery group to learn how to claim
the stranger out there, to feel more to fear less
of what she feels sucking through the house,
through the house of her child's shadow.

"It doesn't have to be like that — does it?"
Gloria shows Alan by retracing the death
that traced itself after her for most of her
adult life, sharing what it was that was
escaping in the evaporating blood of her
broken father she found on the stone pavement,
where he released himself from the roof of his universe
of his six-story University Avenue apartment house,
wrapped in a sheet — just a smudged, scribbled note:
Forgive me, forgive me for this.

Gloria writes it for Alan as someone wrote it for her,
Recovery's last address, where the late wanderers come
to know one another by their scars. Rachelle will see,
as she has seen, "she's not really alone in the woods,
no one makes it truly alone." Out of the vapors
invisibly expanding, out of the sparked heat's

sputter, rising from the hearth and enveloping
a placeless direction from all these homemade maps
toward being, on the volatile road to Recovery,
out of herself there swells an opening in smile,
a flashing across the orange snapping tongues,
from Rachelle to Alan to talk it over again.
Come home, Rachelle, he doesn't say. It would be
too soon to ask her to forgive herself.

After two years of solitaire in his Coney Island room
locked from the inside with peace to readeatshithate,
after years of trying to graduate from it all
in degrees of clinical psychology with a blood-splitting
first that broke the breath through his mother's nose,
only to back out into this fractured world again,
with a Freeman certificate of new name, after years
in miles of Eisman distance, cousin Donald Freeman
has dropped in on this seed-scattering September day.

He puffs up a smoke shield around his onyx eyes
and casts them as stonethrower at each Eisman.
One by one, each is struck — Nemesis is his
to hurl through holes in shredding smoke,
and to hide from behind his shield. He must
keep basting his tongue in wrath's burning leaves,
keep the yellow bitter juice just under his
lashing laughter at Gloria as "the only one who
doesn't know just who led her old man up the stairs,
and wrapped him up in the bedsheet, just what
hand pushed her brother Reis, the Juliard genius,
to drive his music down a circular bus route,
his pathetic score with no beginning, no ending,
just a middle he plays on and on and on,
his unique capacity such a gnawing root of need,
just what hand choked it off in the exhaust fumes —
"a truly Chekhovian sister — loosely speaking,"
he winks at Aunt Ruth. "He'll soon pass a skullcap
around, and all the devoted Eismans will give."

"No one's hands have that kind of push."
Gloria coughs into her own. "Not even hers."
Silently overhead, the ashbreath of all
we've burned intertwines into one smoke
staining the crisscrossed housespine.

It is Donald who notices the maples tower
over their seedlings, sucking away their light,

as he towers over his father Manny, whose
gentleness contained all the butts and sucked out
bones Donald passed out on trays for two years,
half a psychologist, half an Eisman, wholly
something else, reaching out for what
recedes like nebulae when reached out for
through the closed canopy of his room,
reaching in under that canopy for his sister
Beth, finding his father's pilgrimage
began twisting there too, as in these tangled
woods where branches twist up around each other
on the same tree, reaching for the black-chasing sun.

I need a new home,
she had said to me.
It's an emergency.
Her thinwire voice
dropped groundward,
moving like emotion
to be empty of itself.
Each word an overload
squeezed off live,
un-quivered, un-stressed
I have to get out
before Don returns
from Fire Island.

After twenty years Donald asks me who I am.
"Too bad," he says, "that you're my cousin."
I wonder what vague semblance of himself
he winks at in me, what Beth he creates
through his strained smoky stories of his
devotion that forces him to have to live
with his parents at 40 to save his sister
from their mother's overdevotion, that kept
Beth in a crib till 13 — like a bud that opened
brown-petalled, past itself. "I like autumn,"
she says, her eyes full of fear, drawn into
her same drab sweater she wears like numb skin,
in the settee skintight with her mother Deanna
in the same drab sweater. They eat from the same
plate Deanna filled for them, a drab pair,
with their backs to the fire, they turn
onlookers to the twitching flames.

I can't live in that halfway
house where no one knows me,
and I can't just rush out

[46]

for my own strange place.
I'm going home where I belong.

"It's no one's business," Donald hisses
"especially yours, Deanna, just how many times
her date kissed her!" He wanders in and out
of his smoke like a bird through fog that comes
and goes and comes and goes and calls out,
that can't find a resting place for itself
and calls out for all his devotion that doesn't
unscramble the scrambled guidance of electro-therapy
Beth gets on and off to force a charge back into her.

Her anti-depressant giggling blows static
through my hair. She whispers to me,
"It was only once!" at the top of her voice,
where Deanna's arms crisscross — " So he did
kiss you!" — "Bravo for Beth," cheers Deborah,
bouncing her sobbing two-year-old
as she downs three halfspoons of oatmeal
for an ulcer. "He's not for Beth."
Donald shreds a napkin, drops the pieces.
"He can't support her." Manny limps
to the fireplace, tosses in Donald's shreds.

And we are all subdued. What is there to say
that is whole enough in the breath-churned smoke,
in the overhanging echoes of our confusion?
The air quivers with Beth's lackluster giggling
all her people-blocked way to the bathroom's
stonewall sanctuary — and I am of them and not
of them, and each pole of me would be effete
without the other, and there is a nameless interface
I have only glimpsed in stillness when I am
of them and not of them, that I have no map toward,
where the will of inexplicable emotion and the will
to control that will are one, and I am of them
and not of them, and I am inexplicably of me
because I am of them and not of them —

"You're no better!" my mother tells her brother
Manny. "What good's a steady income if you're
steadily blowing it away at the tracks?
How much of it can you really call your own?"

Crying on the ledge of her mommy's pumping knee,
Vickie fails again to be consoled. Deborah, up

[47]

most of the night, asks her father to pick
her up, at whose birth she hid all knives
from the kitchen, unable to ever lift the baby.
Having to eat baby food with her baby,
with knife-sharp pains cutting into her throat
right through her chest, no doctor could explain
with lights dropped down her gullet, searching
for the shape of what couldn't be seen.

Vickie's sobbing fills the room, and in breaker,
breaker after breaker, the current
will not wash out, but catches in her
small chest like a stone she can't cough up
— she gasps — is fed bronchial dilators.

O how the ghostly vapors sputter to rise
with her cry that calls out for place
from within these embedded stones,
where it takes cement to seal a hearth
strong enough to contain such fire.
But what subtle strength is elastic
enough for the heart's containment?

What is it in us that sighs in sympathy
with all the sighing branches, independently
adrift in high currents around this house,
connecting in the underground, one thirst?

What is this unswaddled current that runs
through my family — electrodes to the heads
of my mother, my aunts, my cousins, their temples
burning in valleys of sunken skull, and it is
all around me, I feel them forever receding
through inner woods, dying to stone
dreams where the light cannot reach,
struggling upward for any canopy?

Out of the shadows drawing their definitions
from the flames, as we each take a turn
with the poker and stoke up a volley
of fiery eyes, out of these crackling voices,
I hear my elemental name calling me
to utter what I cannot understand —

Why Ruth's migraine can't consume itself each day.
        "More kindling — chop some more."

Why her daughter went through med school anorexic.
  "But where's its main axis? Hold Vickie."

Why Gloria twice bound a ghost in her arms
in nights' free-floating sanitarium gown,
then just let it go because she owned it.

Why her little Ross was sent so remotely away
to live with the neighbor next door —
why such wide-open desolation is in his eyes.

Why Deborah's arms can't lift to paint nor swim,
bounded in the heaviness of their own strokes.
  "Here, let me haul it."
  "No, it's too much for one person."
  O branched symmetry!

Why Reis purged himself three meals a day
with carrot water for his at-onement.
  "Look, a little skeleton on the wood."
  Must all little creatures prostrate
  themselves before thee, O mighty tree?

Why Hannah can't return from the blank stare
of her manchild who never knows her, can't wipe
off his sticky seed he wiped off on her hand.

Why Beth won't leave the silence
of a cold stone sanctuary.
  "Beth?"
  "Does the door open going out or in?"
  "I don't know."
  "Is she really in there after so long?"
Why my mother scatters x-rays of all
the life she's had to sacrifice to live.

Why I dedicate this burning through this
crude swaddling bark, as if I needed a ritual
to hope for a smoother arbor of the heart
for you, my son, whose endless journey,
like a poem's endless approach toward
integrity has only as always just begun.
  When a tree burns, you set its spirit free.

And why one by one we have come to gather
around this fireplace that releases
a sweetwood fragrance out of crackling.
Escape O raw smoke spirit.
Escape and be whole as sunlight.
Why one by one we have come to warm
our hands in the smoke of what
we've hauled; one by one we have come,
if only for this moment, godless yet unalone,
unritualized yet sanctified by a sharing;
one by one we have come for the at-onement
in never knowing our own snared heat because
we fear the burning that doesn't consume.
Gloria opens the sealed pod of the piano.
Manny hums what she strikes with hammers.
Escape O raw smoke spirit.
Escape and be whole as sunlight.
Why one by one we have come for the at-
onement in embracing all that we can
that we fear that we are under this,
our close canopy of the night,
where like the countless petrified stones
we're immobilized over the edges
of our graves haunted by life.
Beth edges herself onto the needlepoint
cushion at the piano, squints at some music
in her hand. And as a melody's moment
seeps through the time-tremulous air,
and Vickie crawls through the set legs
Ruth and Hannah unfold to touch at
the tempo of the song with their toes,
and as one by one we have come for
the at-onement inglowing orange-flashes
on the hearth's horizon, why now
Manny swallows the stone in his throat
and opens fullsonged for us all.

The Sunflower

I think it was when I found the decapitated stalk
 that I remembered how I learned to grow
my flowers indoors, on the body of my dead parakeet,
 in an 8-inch cheesebox with 3 inches of soil
scooped from the weedy fringe of a community lot,
 where boisterous little leaguers struck
 out for the beauty and terror anew.

Nothing but a bizarre weed would grow in that box
 and prolific mites casting webs of dark
tensions beneath the leaves, cut-off from circulation
 of earth minerals. I remembered, from the east
sill to the west sill, as I kept moving my weed, still
 how hard it was to hold the light indoors —
yet that weed unabashedly bloomed one morning, a minute
 lavender I thought slipped from the breast
 of my parakeet thaumaturge, Pretty Boy.

When my father visited one afternoon last summer
 we sat on sunchairs in the garden
beneath that big, petalled sun's-eye view,
 Paul's only surviving sunflower,
that he'd hoed and weeded up to his window height,
 bringing a yellower light into his room.
Funny how at its height it seemed most burdened ·
 with the weight of its own beauty
and hunched itself inward like an old pundit
 on a sturdy stalk of vast heart -
 shaped leaves for shade

We waved to my neighbors in their garden over a root-
 hung fence, where roses and their teenage boy
were doing their earthwork and rising in bright sun,
 outgrowing the wattled security there.
Hunched-in on his own center of secrets, my father
 asked me questions he knew the answers to,
not out of false humility, but to hide what mattered
 to him, or to preserve what had taken him
his life to know he knew. He asked me if I knew
 why that handsome boy so often wore
 a gawky cap so low on his face.

I told him what I knew about when their boy was seven,
    a little younger than Paul, with a head
of copious ringlets, golden as corn silk, how just
    about when boys grow strangely aware
of themselves, and he was prattling over some immense
    escapade of his, two men yanked him
by his hair down the backstairs behind the movies,
    shaved off his boyhood curls, and as they
made him drop his pants, they made him retch
    down his hair so he'd never forget
        the initiation into his beauty

My father warned me how intolerable the sunlight,
    his grandson shouldn't saunter off
in it. I thought I could never ask Paul to
    ensconce his flowers in a cheesebox
with a plastic's pure soil, nor to try
    to balance a box of transient sun
        on such a narrow sill.

My father's face was more parchment than before,
    tan-wizened, bald-pated like an old
sunflower disk not yet ready to release its seeds
    that weighted it, shorter, but riper
than before. Space shrank before his eyes
    as I watched him fall into himself,
        into his own heavy memories.

Whoever it was must have come late at night,
    when boundaries get swallowed whole,
whoever it was must have brought a saw,
    or an ax, and hacked hard to spirit
off that unripened disk that wouldn't grow
    on anyone else's stalk
        but Paul's.

Processional

Planted by wind or whim or what have you
    at the base of his schoolyard fence,
where I often sat waiting with apples and mufflers
    for him, feeling sorry for these burgeoning
contortions of feathery leaflets
    twisting their way through catenate iron, the young
mimosa grew where even open space seemed bound
    by the terms of metal boxes around the play area,
something like his learning to fit
    his words between the measured spaces on a page.

I watched him make his lickerish wishes
    on its fuzzy pink globes. How silently some branch
would lift a piece of fence right up
    to make room for its own mute mettle,
something of the way his thought in its passage
    would sometimes lift the language right out
from its ground, or something of the way a poem
    pushes to grow out from under its metaphor.
But what it couldn't lift, nor contort its growing
    being through, those most rigid wires,

"it's eaten," he said and pointed to where
    the wire disappeared inside the wood.
"But if we could look inside," I said,
    "I bet its wires would show."
Unlike all those stacked primers he carried —
    each year heavier than the last —
those readable and those not that would untenably
    dissolve with him again and again, an unreachable
yet familiar surprise to me in his flight
    of answers to his own stark questions.

And are there deeper regions in him still,
    some pristine impenetrable expanse of being?
In the procession I remember how
    he walked up front with his father
and I behind with mine on the Day of Atonement,
    a chain of generations en route
to temple, the three in their dark, linty suits.
    I worried how he would take in
those hard knuckles full of sin, that rigid,
    abstract cadence on the chest

of my father, knocking on the chest
of his father, with frontlets between their eyes,
whether he'd hear it or not, he'd hear it,
he'd hear it, his ears never close.
"I'm never so sure what my sins are
but sometimes I forgive them
and sometimes I relive them. I guess
I know no sure-fire techniques,"
I tried again to explain myself to my father
who had affixed heathen epithets to his own

name in me a lifetime ago.
They had their prayer shawls, their tickets,
his open hand. I walked back alone
and sat alone under this tree
looking for atonement because I was no Solomon,
because I couldn't divide him
to be neither mine nor yours.
Now that he's been Bar Mitzvahed,
it's no longer clear what holds what up.
At the intersection of what fence got lifted

and what fence was not, is the crooked and kinked
ineffable shape of this one mimosa.
What equanimity to engulf what would not
budge, to internalize, but not
to merge, to retain that original
pith within.
It's never considered moving out
from under its fence any more than he's
ever asked for a new alphabet.
But it's never writhed in its roots

to cast out that iron god in its veins.
No one's ever branded it a heathen
nor refused to speak its name
for having no sins to throw away,
and no one's ever forgiven it its uniqueness
nor needed to.
And while we've played together around it, searching
for secret breakthroughs to the other side,
it's never wrested with its mute possession of space
while its saplings warp up along the far fence.

The Intersection of Two Men

"Here is your Hebrew prayer primer you pissed on, Mr. Orthodox,
who keeps non-kosher meat in his bed.

"Here's your accordion I wasted my money on, sealed-up in a box
for 15 years with your hotshot music that fattened the roaches.

"Your blank book I blew 5 bucks on to prove to you you couldn't
fill up a novel. I did what I had to to raise you to yourself.

"Your caved-in bed where you assumed your most productive position
—take it with you and your backside dreams. I couldn't rest on
your lumps. She'd've straightened and bronzed it.

"Dog tag, military uniform, bar mitzvah yarmulke, your sunken sack
of stories—in other words, your meal tickets, since, Free-Loader,
you won't be belching off your hot air here anymore.

"What's this? Your first report card, the last you got S° on—so,
Mr. S°S°, look at—from high school—my very own signatures
in your very own handwriting. Your flunk-out letter from Cornell.
Maybe you could laminate it like a diploma, Mr. Office Temporary.

"Well, the $30 orthopedic bar she couldn't bear to restrain you in.
'Let him walk turned in!' she hollered. 'It's barbaric to bind him.
Life's shackle enough!' No wonder you're going nowhere, no wonder
you're always walking turned-in, Mr. World-Owes-You-A-Living.

"And what about your case of microscope slides? Remember—heh!—
how you compared our fingerprints for differences? What? Why
you still poring over me like a smug FBI man? I know how you think!
Yes, they'd be all over her—outside, inside, my fool fingerprints.

"This too? Stale bag of sunflower seeds she infected you with.
Too late—too late to cure you, she had it too—Non-Contenders—
nothing's more infuriating than the low punches of a woman who will
not fight! Take it—wishing-well she pasted-up from your ice-cream
sticks, discolored dust collector. Its pennies can keep you afloat.

"Let me—O—puzzle, that abstract you lived on, all 3000 pieces,
all the same no matter how you turn it. That was the year I wasn't
Plato enough to talk to. Remember? Mr. KantWasteWordsOnMiniminds.
Broke her up each time you harangued her with Kant—she hid it—
yep! and can't open the eyes of a Neanderthal like me, right?
Or your own before noon—can't show him colors with the inches
on his ruler!—but we know the color of your inch-ruler, right?

[55]

"Pack up all these trophies, Mr. Basketball, Mr. Horseback.
Won't spitshine them for you like she did—you'll always be her
Lone Ranger, all saddled up there with your spanking clean spurs
of sanctimony. None of us ordinary people get trophies after 18.
What the? I don't believe—she saved all this wood—deadwood—
scraps—no two pieces the same. Damn, don't even fit together.
No wonder I had no closet space to call my own between you.

"Do you believe her! Why not hold on to every damned band-aid,
every damned toothpick that ever touched the ivory of her baby
—your dental retainer, sir. Held up the tusks y'got from sucking
so long. Your bite ever straighten out? Eh, what difference from
what angle a bite comes? A bite is a bite. A bite by any other
wouldn't hurt as much, Mr. Silent-Movie? A whole year not talking
to me, a whole year she blamed me you only talk to her—God, why
must we got through all this? Why couldn't she throw anything away?

"Old junk! Fossils! Underground-Schemer! She planned this too.
She knew—she knew one day we'd have to dig through all this junk
together—piece by piece like fool archeologists—fool woman!
It won't work. Hoarder!—I can't—I don't have the patience. Fool.
Like the damned Passover she cried us into talking again—no—no,
she was always revengeful. Fool-Quiet woman. This is my punishment
for all the years I didn't help clean up, let it all accumulate—
I'm so tired—so tired. Give it up—give it up already. Got to go
lie down. Mr. Crybaby, help me clear off this hodgepodge here
on my bed. Eh, leave it. Too much to move. I should try your lumps
—Heh! She'd have her revenge after all—Silent Partners, yep,
Conspirators, the two'v you—there—over there, my address—there—

"What? Dark already? Eh, what's the sense to look back so far.
My eyes hurt. Hold it up so I can see it. Yisgadal Veyiskadash—
I used to look for her at Rockaway—her head in the bathing cap—
she swam out so far I couldn't follow her bobbing dot in the waves
—like the dot underneath the words to a song she'd sing with TV—
I could never keep up with that dot—y'know—Sh'may Rabbo Be'olmo
Deevro Chiroosey Ve'yamlich—I'm so tired—so tired—you take
what you want—take it all—I'm not a junk man—I'm not."

Jack-O'-Lanterns at Their Doors

They flock together in an endless chain, extending themselves
all the way across Pelham Parkway on blistered wood benches,
the elderly Jews in felt hats, blotting up sun, and lambskin
toppers, puffing out their chests with cigars and talk
of their children. Another harvest of light is almost through.
The trees have rusted around them. Like the pigeons, they
have come for the sun and the gathering of their kind
on this shortgrowing fall day, as they bicker over who
sits where in the sun. Ready to defend themselves, they come
armed with parched snapshots their clicking cameras shed
like yellow leaves, and laminations of what their children
made them, and their children's children broken SWAK seals.

They are the family historians, the narrators of the Bronx romance.
As the wax is gathered in their ears — sealing them in —
with a rush of blood come nutrients washed up from beneath
— kosher pickles swimming in the spiced barrel eyes of a child
— Moishe's pushcart — lunch apples for a nickel — riding free
and sockless — standing in the moving Westchester Avenue trolley
— hitchhiking the night away up West Farms Road — holding money
in your open hands in the open air — the *Forward* reading
backward on a slow-shuttered reel of an autumn afternoon.

With hands that interrupt the tremors of the linden trees,
1/4 in English, 3/4 in Yiddish, the story gets told on some
Parkway bench every sunny afternoon, winked at by a grandchild
every last Sunday of the month. O the way their Bronx was.
Their eyes move back and forth on nothing more than sunthreads,
as if under some mobile swinging linked shapes to hold — to hold
— to stare — to grasp — to sleep — to sleep — to shuttle back along
darker tracks — rattling and banging with sense-chafing blasts
they don't tell the grandchildren about, except as gentle tales
of subterranean afternoons riding without reason, nor need
for one, back and forth, back and forth on the 42nd St. shuttle.

Yarmulkes and kerchiefs have absorbed lost colors of their hair,
colors they find again stained in glass in the shul, burning
slowly through the leaves. The Yahrzeit candle glows indifferent
to their debates — "My mother, may she rest in peace, has always
looked down on me," sighs Emma, her head shaking involuntarily.
"And is she with her mother who is with her mother who is
with her mother and so on and so on back to Eve?" mocks Aaron.

Lidded pillowboxes dangle in their time-measured wholeness
in powdered grains, deep in their pockets, where all the loves
of their lives suddenly pulverize into a moment's warmth
on a bench in the sun. In this living so long on Pelham Pkwy.,
they have come to mimic the local trees — some have bristles
and spines, and some are S-shaped and bare, their limbs are
freeing to themselves again, their work is done, the draining
radiance is sinking into itself. And some have come to scatter
crusts, whistling for feathers that flutter from beyond
the split branches — "Here Mercury! Here Snowflake! Oooo —
did you think I wouldn't come for you today? Mama's here."

I find the bench where my grandmother used to display her
hundred-hour volunteer buttons and badges, gold-winged service
pins for her twenty years at the Beth Abraham Home for unwanted
incurables, spoonfeeding the armless, sponging the listless.
A man with hyaline eyes offers me a seat — "Life is like
a hydra," he philosophizes with both hands. "You cut off one
problem, a new one grows." I try to follow, through his
articulate fingers, the indelible number on his wrist, and white
bandages around his ankles, that are swollen and deadlocked
like all his chrysalis lives that never hatched in his spring.
His children are cruising the Mediterranean out of Piraeus —
"getting their dollar's worth in drachmas and baklava!" —

She spoke with both hands too — of red jelly-filled candies —
large bow tie cookies — hand-woven baskets for bread — raisins
spilling over from coffee tins — and even then in her flower-
print robe that loosened away from her body — she held out
the double cartons of orange juice she stashed for us
from the nursing home pilferers in case we were thirsty —

He advises me to keep some money in a Swiss bank as he
recalls 5000 marks slipped as an offering into a taylor's
slammed books — " 'Nicht genug!' Think it can't happen here?"
We watch the wind herd the clouds across the Parkway sky
like some vast seasonal migration. A room with a view
of the Parkway is a blessing when that certain white light
breaks rainbow upon each wound in the glass, and the stained
window opens out upon this little grass island, surrounded
by an asphalt sea, a faint redolence of a distant skin burning.

Doing a push-up off his mahogany cane, a man stakes his place
in the migration of canes across the Parkway. Leaves crack
to mosaic bits under his feet as he goes with a friend
for a little strolling, on a wide open, grandchild-fringed
road. They welcome the level places, touch-up piecemeal
assortments from family dramas in the arcade that's never
out of season — it's a trip within a trip . . . .

Against the falling leaf, the wider horizon, the crisp rustle
of a newly fallen friend, a man's pace changes. He can pause now
to think some thoughts unbounded by the height of the stock
market, or the brown of a woman's eyes. For time has swelled
like the gourd, detaching from the vine, carving itself
into the most grotesque jack-o'-lantern of all.

White frosted mornings vanish with grandchildren, and whispery
autumn evenings seep into their rooms. Every evening now,
the stars of eternity are more in their places, more clearly
seen as the leaves snap from under the wax of unopened buds,
waiting on another spring. While all the eaves along the Parkway
moan a memento mori, a seat in the warm open air in this
haunted month of Halloween is a seat up front on a high holy day.

More Than He Knew

At her window shrine, the snake is alive
but does not hiss, and the prayer is alive
but spotted and wordless. The spider god
has no ears and hangs weaving with light

above, keeping the prayer in the dark,
clasping itself. Her shrine is here,
an aimless aloneness with objects she
cultivates to bemind her — she enters

the sorrowful wisdom in the familiar stone
eyes of the hoary black man. His beard
is as spotted with white as her father's
old face is spotted with black, the color

he taught her to roll-up windows fast
'from, as they drove through Harlem
when she was a child. Now he prays
for her health in his temple. At home,

she stares at what he could touch only
in stone in a statue, till the after-image
of his gift is her father's old, sweet face —
how he had ministered to so many of the myriad

meanderings of her hopes' streaming ways,
yes, that was how, how he could raise
a loaded stone, like a prophet on the water
in her eye, yes, that was how he made

it move as a delicate softness through walls
around her heart, as she had entered
the tattered hallway to tutor a girl
against his lesser judgment, and arrived

at eighteen. Yes, that was how, though she
could never tell him so, it's enough somehow
she understands, as she waters her shrine,
how he had taught her more than he knew.

Patchwork

He was tucking her in.
He gathered to kiss
his handful of sand
to throw to her.
A handful of cloud
remained. Being
nineteen, he tried
to follow the seams
as if those of his mother's
caring could be kept
straight. His breath
surrendered as she, still
bending over him, a kiss
and a fuzzy patchwork
for a small boy, under
the strain, shovelful
by shovelful, no way
to lade love back,
this heap irreducible,
his manhood perspective
swelling with her blood
as she'd swelled with his,
this lifetime effort
to return each grain
he missed — scraped up.
One uncle charged the other's
Helplessness with *Indifference*
and cried, "That's enough!"
and tried to hold her
son. But he shovelled
More sand. More sand.
Into the opening that was
her bed, each heaving
of sand in the orthodox
way, his labor pain
of undoing such
a Sisyphean Load.

Old Woman's Plot

White marble chips are her ground
she parts for peat moss, rich black humus,
the perennial remembering of a future
pinkyellow-rayed, deepset red-haloed,

day's double eye about to reopen to her
amethyst bubble of volcano. (The Greeks,
she read, believed the stone and plant
of that name could keep you sober.)

A solidified burning she juxtaposed
to the new gaillardia seeds, little
shuttlecocks from her hand to the land.
Sunflashing mica eyes she positioned

over her sinuous gully she filled with smooth
turquoise gravel, her solid Caribbean Sea
water unmoving, better than real, attracts
no bugs to her white gypsophila, baby's breath,

breath of feathers staked and named. Still,
it's the part she can't contain she loves
the best in spite of all its unruliness.
A slice of geode from Mexico, a dried overspill

of Indian paint pot, a granite piece
of Yosemite at the foot of the bridge
washed with California redwood stain.
Every stone has a thousand eyes:

this from the Bahama marketplace at the dock —
How much you want to pay for seastone, pretty lady?
with chip on bottom. *You hold upside down;*
this old brown fish rock

hole held gill breathings, now empty
gills of afternoon breathing through
her wishing well, home of a million feet
that come and go: these red-winged blackbird feet

she knows; these slimy slug trails
she can name, but others skulk beneath
her bright coral fan. Star-leaf lupines
are long pink lighthouses whose petals

point out the sun and the stars
to the stone duck on the white marble shore,
beak in arched wing, never swims away from its spot.
Correspondences of rose petals and rose quartz,

tiger lily and tiger eye, so each
staked-up bender aligns for her with its
unmovable twin. Only the wind finds
their corresponding faults. She breathes

a white lime cloud, diazinon
genocide side of beauty in her lungs,
rubs vaseline on the rocks to preserve
the wet look of the sea in a lone

achieved stillness on her knees.
Sere of succession and sere of withering
in one word, it's all contained
without a fence, open to all to see

her succession of bloomings she's timed,
keeps beauty as long as she can.
Till frost yellow coreopses keep opening
one after another. The transparent quartz design

she can see clear through to the ground
with her one good eye. Only the shadows
sweep the sharpnesses unbruised.
Her hands are all cut up, dirt fills each wound

so ugly to make it lovely here where
there's no place to walk on this bridge,
no water to drink, no fruit to eat,
nothing useful is beautiful to her.

What Is the Radiance of the Ice?

On the pane, the ice imprisons
a stark cold
resplendence, an aurous riddle.

I hold heat to the ice tentacles
stinging through
my leg and abdomen. I am

immobilized for 3 weeks of Now —
or longer —
by an old familiar friend,

an inhering man-of-war.
He is my
enrapturer of exposed nerve.

He knows no distinction of sorrows,
but entwines
your sultry kiss right through

the injury to my constricted muscle,
the ice of isolation
right through the radiance of your eyes,

frozen-over, till I am One —
and it seems
I have always been splayed here

waiting for something to heal —
and what
does it mean, to heal, if not

to paralyze and devour such old
imprisoning cells?
As I am unmoved in spacetime,

the new, new physics book tells me
I am all
motion, zero motion is absolute motion,

and time must stop for them both —
intoxicated
with so much wakefulness, I am

sweating love's liquid clarity
under the reciprocity
of the sky and your heartbeat,

by the outside-opening window,
our undulations
radiate everywhere through the charged

dust of other lovers in the air —
and the cold
opaque eyes are other windows

waiting across the wide, dismal
way with their
outstretched sills like funnels —

and I wake loving you, not
again, not
as then, but Now, that's the koan —

What is the love that defies
separation,
the superluminal connection of two

individuals once intimate in interaction,
the riddle
even Einstein couldn't explain?

What is that sudden charge
of your *Jerusalem*
refrain in silence that is never pure?

What is that certain tilt
of your poetics
in the slanting flood from my pen?

What is that sourceless spinning,
that newness our
togetherness weaves as we move ever further apart?

The Calling

When I am whispering within
thin birdclung strands, stringing
out for you, quivering, to be heard,
or that I will be heard, after so many
báckroads wedge between us,
will you receive my unspoken vibration?
Up the breath-ripping switchback,
to be honest, to utter need,

will each word be just static
across the distance? I believe
the heart's energy is never destroyed —
it's unforgivable how we can hear it
just the same. There's a humming over
the honk-cursing expresswayers that we are,
over our crashings into each other's
slick rainbows. Through this stretch

of smoke along the highway, the vagaries
of our weather, flash floods, wash out —
I need you to know that I'm all right,
past the shock and the circuit of denial.
Whatever voice survives this ordeal
to get through to you, lingers still,
strung up on air somewhere —
like in a high wire act between New York

and San Diego, waiting, stung by a yellow
fullness of that energy over a field gone
to seed and ice. Wild bittersweet twistings
we clipped in fullness hang on, love,
to that field in a dusty, dry vase.
More than words fail emotion,
emotion makes words fail. When I was 10,
I could laugh a long time on a string

between frozen juice cans — hello and goodby
held slacker then. There's a peregrine
whistling within my windy line, a haunting
of all we never say that's never lost.
So much is left dangling by this thread
over dammed water, too dry to speak,
a whole forest creaking, a boarded-up cabin
suspended across a time-zone, snagged

across a trail of words like discordant weeds —
I could hang up. There are other journeys
made without cords. Once, out of the radiant
edge of darkness, in serenity, a dear friend
returned her childhood glance to me
from her writing desk in our old grade school,
where we were always in the same class together.
Long years of estrangement were irrelevant

in her quiet eyes, and there were no foolish
words strung out toward our grown-up loss
of each other, for they had not yet been said.
Everything was the same in all that time.
We would always be approaching summer vacation
in the stillness, and its fullness meant
loss as always. She brought her sadness up
to my future eyes. I bent down the years

to tell the little girl I would see her again,
without a word, without the letter I mailed
to her uncertain address. We knew. And when
she called, we both cried that there had been
another calling, a calling from ending,
a calling from the dying of her mother,
and she in her loss had dreamt awake our childhood
to help her sleep, when I was dreaming our childhood

in sleep to help me awake. We knew the calling.
Somewhere within our urgencies, we coincide,
we are the wordless stillness within the eye
of our storm, we keep of each other,
we belong to no years. There's a groaning
in the overloaded line, as if suddenly,
having to say it all in three minutes of years,
I can hear so many voices straining and sighing,

tossed down abysmal fields, each with a weather-
eaten house, invaded by doorweeds that thrive
in connections. Each ghost town is another
person's home, each knowing his own isolation,
here where I linger with the wheat's murmuring
in a waving of lost voices ripe with need,
here where heart country is an aeolian harp
of strings sounded and shaped by currents

stretching from everywhichway, from cacophonous
wind, from inmost squall, the unison is tuned
in a frailest pianissimo, in the strings
in the air. What we mean to each other is caught
up in some Main Street wind with its fast food
vibrations. Learning new names, dialing
new numbers, to say the same thing to each other,
though you say you are finished when I've just

begun, we keep of each other. Listen
beneath our words for the same nameless
hummings. Some moments we belong to no years
when I know your tremolo inheres in mine,
when your lunar songs come back my unspoken
other side, when a vibrance of you pierces
through my long, dark punctuations, when I know
I am not just the calling and receiving

of my own urgency, like a static cry trapped
inside an unread poem, though you hear
but a humming across unspeakable country distances,
where I've journeyed so far not to say
what comes whispering through your sleep,
a spelling, a lulling, some ancient and familiar
song of that spillage of life, O love, from within,
softly playing across your own throbbing strings.

Behind the Glass Door with My Cat

My Twinkle has used up eight lives:
one flowed out his gash from a flowering
branch he went leaping for; three drained out
his abscesses from testing the turf's fangs,
all leaping toward the same slope of sun;
one splintered beneath a brakeless driver
as Twinkle went leaping for his Tania
prancing on her parallel driveway; one just
dissolved into the floor where he lay

after neutering; and two must have been lost
in the middle of more subtle, mellower leaps
out toward whatever moves around out there,
because the vet said this is Twinkle's last one:
indoors. It's for his own good, this boundary,
I suppose, every theory of life must specify.
As I write a love poem to you, I hear him cry
at the fire-engine, spring geranium, the swelling
grass, proffering glassed wings, juiceless stamens,

and a life of logical fallacy, an oversimplified
either/or: to sleep or to leap at the closed
door he can see through to what he can't
have. When Tania scratches at the glass,
he scratches back, trips the alarm string
to ring like a siren through my poem — I leap
at the many lusters of your laughter,
reset the net of moonlight in your arms,
nurture your praise like a psalm.

I've strived for the clarity of a glass
door disposition, I've strived to envision
clear through to how you can only survive
behind it —
It's for the best, I tell myself,
I don't know where you are — I don't want
to know — It's for the best — I suppose,
beyond these lines —

My Sister and I in Storm

[F o r   P a t]

Swaying out on the ultimate
wind-whipped cornice . . . .
WH AUDEN

We wake from weightless dreams to a violence
in the sand/ that lashes at our eyes/ the sudden
floodback of our losses/ We keep barred
entrances to each other/ as we lie at the risen
sea and stagnate in that long/ hurtful moment/
strangers in our separate backwaters/ till she
speaks to me about the forecasters/ who must
predict with an upside-down divining rod/
She raises a smile/ and about her baby
who would have been a baby boy/ Electro-
denunciations are hurled around the rescuers
who clear the calm-slashed resting place/
for the swarthy/ swaggering majesties
of scorchfire and colorless milk/ we curse
then welcome to divest ourselves of our
gauze robes/ and cushioned shoes/
We open our palms to the slashing cold/
to the scorching fear/ We open our mouths
to the torrential bacchanal/ We yoke arms
and we dance for the hectors of the universe/
We ask each other why/ we're doing this
without intent to stop/ Our dithyrambic
movements on the sand leave hieroglyphics/
as from two wild feather droppers/ even we
cannot decipher this devotion to the charged
emotion/ What penetrates our pores/ razes
our turrets/ we built knowing we'd lose/

Under a leaking awning/ where a few rescuers
hang around/ hieratic to a few young
bikinied girls/ shivering/ we sip
hot tea and talk personal chowder/
We give our words as tethers/ to each other
and hold on tighter to the soaked blanket
we share/ We sit enticed by horizonal homage/
how thin the grizzly line that stretches

[70]

across everything/ how many tossed
to the same lead prongs of ancient tridents/
"Look/ you can see why they called it flat"
she says/ "You have to get up high/
higher than a mountain/ high as an astronaut
to see the ocean like a pond/ curving
back on itself" And as she speaks I wonder/
will we ever get up high enough
to see a curving back/ or will we
always be ancient seafarers/ overhanging
a flat drop-off into leaden silence/

A December Morning Decision

Upleaping intruders, two squirrels
in my torpor over coffee,
6 am, and they can capriole
from the tangled, branched dark.
They set their trembling brazenness
on a slit of light at my sill
and wait their due in the pose of monks.
They flick their fanned tails
close over their backs
and their hairs align
under the northwind's magnet.
I lumber to them with a fistful
of nuts and raisins and annoyance
at having to move myself at all.
Across the arcane iced glass,
nose to nose
with the winsome, white tufted one,
my favorite, whose unmatched feats include
vaulting off with two peanuts at once —
shoves the first way back in his mouth
with the second's snap just under the teeth —
and shimmying up the birdfeeder pole
to rout out the sunflower seeds.
Looking in, he lingers on the sill
and over his peanuts, splitting them
as if he had earned them,
while I, looking out, resolve to linger
over this coffee and over this day,
accepting all its offerings
and to feel entitled to them.

A Hair's Breath

It's got no bounce, no curl, no shape at all,
no windswept wave, just won't behave — a real
pity she sighed for her round-faced girl,
a pity it's hard to resist what you're told's a big deal,

that you've got only 4 hairs when you were only 6 years,
And it was elementary arithmetic to count them out loud
and cut them down into bangs, to cloud up their air
with ammonia fumes and heated oil, to pull them ouch-

tight around toothed-rubber clamps, so some
permanent chemical remains long years through washings,
after long split-end days of school-chum fun
you'd swallowed-the-box-of-Brillo teasings,

till you're old enough to do the teasings yourself
with a bristle brush and your head upside down.
You scuff up the spirit of Static, and your yelp,
through your hair — damn! — then yank it around and around

4 megarollers on which you dream crook-necked dreams . . .
You wake to shake out your inadequate frizziness
and lacquer it all up like stiff, chafed antennae
that even without wind sense life's certain uneasiness.

One lilac Mother's Day you're 40, the whole family's at the park,
your sister whistles a familiar tune as she skims
through your temples for grey, but only finds the dark,
so she suggests you get your hair trimmed,

and your mother agrees you should keep it real short,
to which you retort you'll cut down your hair
when they lose 10 pounds apiece, in a kind of sport.
Triumphantly, your sister says it'd be worth it! Then — despair,

the kind that exposes how lonely the lightning that plays
in shadows and shoots across the frail edges of hair.
Not that the cut was a threat. You knew you were safe.
And no matter who lost or gained, you loved the pair.

But what hurt most was that you so knew the tune
and yet you used it, that subtly pitched pierce
passersby couldn't hear. And all that wishbone afternoon,
junglegym in view, in your laughter, you spied something fierce.

Gagging on regurgitated hairballs is the way
of your cat. He can't stop licking his coat.
But resolving in your combing just before the grey
to not split hairs, to not tease by rote,

to stroke with gentleness, you let your hair breathe
naturally, and it's actually finding its own wave.
But was "straight as sticks" really meant as you believed?
Today, did your mother really say, "I like your hair that way"?

Passover Caribbe

Thank you Emperor
for showing me my lungs
aloud through my ears as never before, for this
new dimension, learning by forgetting
what I had a nose for. If I forgot
to forget what I knew, I'd choke on my habit
of breath that had worked well
for me for some 37 years.
Shiny ebony boy about 19,
long fat braids bursting across your head,
sweet like the black pineapple
fat ladies balanced in braided palm
baskets still green on their heads —
the hummingbird wings whisking

across 15 steel drums, the trade wind
teaching the palms to sing its song,
the hibiscus yellow breasts ringing in banana leaves,
liting to feed from my braided breakfast mat,
and the taste of banana-baked grouper
all feeding into that rippling
where you looked up from under the glass bottom.
"I'm the Emperor," you grinned.
I know why we sailed your name
between the jagged reefs.
"Whoever is chicken man have to pay twice."
You laughed, I would have to pay twice.
And triple for the high-collared, complaining lady.
"This is my garden," you beamed
and gave yourself to its swaying
sea fan, anemone pulse,
your flippers beating between
bright lavender lives,
your snorkel spouting like a porpoise
from the deep, from the whole sea's breathing
motion. Teach me that abandon.

Ashore, we passed the sugar mill stumps
overgrown with vines
dipping into the salt water. Your bitter herbs.
Your great-grandfather beaten and broken
to make the land taste sweet.
We drove you home
to the eaten wooden box, turquoise splashed
on lopsided cinderblocks, a scrawny goat nursing
by a runnel of fetid water.
Never off the island
and you didn't intend to leave your garden
where you had taken the mouthpiece
from your mouth and put it into mine,
taught me to breathe with my ears,
to see with ripples, how
across your breathing batik curtain,
Emperor, we were all descendants of slaves
on that boat, in one direction or another,
without a ritual to learn to breathe
deeper through the other.

The Jogger and the Worm

          Whatever that incipient wind
shakes in the runner's stagnant and stumbling
ease out into the blast of summer sun and black
crow, dove moan and sheer drop from an edge of
a gorge that sings a vibrant and high-fluted
wike wike wike krrrrr entrance, entrance —
begins out of sheer breath, heavy as her limbs
at her blast of will

          to get it going already.
There's the smack of a worm wrestling itself
on its sunsilvered filament of dangling guttrack
with all that self-extending just seeming
so aimless in its swinging at the intricate
dips of oak branch, that sways at the mindless
convolutions of wind, that whirrs at the ongoing
axis of the world,

          that smacks the worm into
the branching feelers of her face to idly dangle
on some sticky strand of her conception. As she
carries it through the jay-flung mulberries that
seed her canvas shoes, she moves with abandoned
sense of loose attention. Does the worm feel it
moves itself or sense her movement any more than
she the earth's as

          it carries her? Oh forget it,
drop that pest, that parasite of particularity
with its appetite for everything in sight. Run
free. Run free. But somewhere between the curve
of the stone and her instep bone, between the
curve of the sagging street and the clasp of
familiar houses with their swinging children
and topiary contrap-

          tions, between the curve of
a day's hopes and tensions and the majestic
maple's sweep-up of what it was from its ground,
making a sweet fluid from that, as she sweeps
across that crisp flow of dead brash breaking up
underfoot, and her body glides deeper into its
element of mind, it emerges in a flash-second
link-up aglimmering,

                        pattern's insinuating thread
winding around the afternoon like a sun-silvered
chrysalis woven of neighbors and strangers left
dangling from voices, as bits and pieces tread
and thread together to a heat expanding to a
bloody self-assertion grasped in that wide
draw of the heart on its stream of debris, all
is dazzlement born

                        of undulant motion, and even
if everything is transforming faster than she
can ever conceive, and every chemical study
of the blood of the motion of the mind
is archaic, and even if understanding always
comes too late, in this treadmill motion is the
luminous instant of catching up when even breath
believes in the

                        elysian knot of the human,
and inhalation and exhalation are one sweet
ensweepment, when the nomadic blood knows itself
most true to its 70,000 miles of vessel track
traversed each day, a third the way to the moon,
cresting waves in the being and assuaging
with the waves' implacable motion, when all
is salty and sure

                        within this glistening, she
is salt lick to an intimate wind, emerging
on the wing of the curve of her anklebone,
and she will not question where the winged worm
flits when cut loose from its continuous strand,
like metaphor broken by some supernal silence
when her being sheds the shape of the wing and
the shape ungrasped,

        and sheds photon after
photon and idly catches them again into its dark
fullness for no reason, a stillness within
the motion. Barbed wire all along the road
around the Grumman Aerospace and Missile Plant
pierces consciousness with the sharpness in her
knee and her weariness. In an awful blast of a
passing train, she

                shudders, what hungers are
wrenching at our strands between all heavens and
earth? what dream so easily moves into belief?
what snake of power slips 'n lisps in our blood?
a half-dead worm in her pocket.

Hedge Pruning and Distractions

Pulling me toward it, as in a fast-forward
motion of the maple's main trunk, this morning
strong sun draws even the uneven edges
of small leaves into purpose, and I stretch up
and out of my bed, reach for the electric
shears, and sense the sheer warmth of task
in its structure in a fire of spring up my spine.

This is the grace of line that whirrs
its matter into the privet's white flowers
releasing their intoxicating power like wee
lungs unladening in song. This is the sweet
scent of shape's desire, the sculptor's skinned
edge, as definitive and ancient as its lonely
trail, for loneliness in its poise is the true

medium of beauty — leaning through a low rumbling,
plunking, thrum, boom from his window, my son shouts
for help with his essay. My shaper yields to his
search for a thesis in the disarming clasp
the Mayan beggar woman gave his hand in Cancun —
then resumes its line somewhat off-kilter.
Yet within the arms clasped to a line

of other arms, like a set of nesting clasps,
one breeding within the other, my shaper
shimmies across a defiant, dry straggler
and seams the non-living branch to the living,
the brittle umber sliding into the curve of green —
to a halt at the telephone's shrill song
and my sister's fretfulness on vacation in Jersey

that she inadvertently left Mr. Coffee plugged in,
and it takes me more than an hour's drive
toward her vision of fire, entrusted with its key —
and back to where the light floats its tracery
in-and-out of my rough hedge in perpetual transformation —
Whirring her way over to me on her electric
wheel chair, my neighbor Blanche, who lives alone,

brakes her strolling wheels and my eager shears
to schmooze awhile. I tell her how good it is
to see her out now that the snows are gone,
and she responds how her son, who practices
art therapy across the country, as a newsboy
brought home an armful of flowers
from a woman on his route, now long dead,

who would become Blanche's friend, who could so
balance the need for acid with the need for base
that lilacs and viburnum bloomed side by side,
one art not interfering but enhancing the other's
flowering was her artistry. In procession
Blanche's other friends come skimming their abundant
absences across my idle blade, and splash

fluidity onto her tongue. My husband calls to me
from the window that my mother is on the phone,
and I know by his tone it's a lie
for the sake of my aching shaper. I go
inside, and cut off her stories in flower,
but without their full release, without
there ever being such a generous possibility,

I console myself to cut my guilty lines
through the raggedy living and the dead edges
of my little yard's hedge, and it has taken me
all day to shape it this uneven way. Looking through
hemlock holes sculpted by scale, Flo calls me
across our street to see, I see my hedge around where
I live, and from here, the gaps have more give.

Freshman Composition

[For EG 11 W1449, Temp II, Western Campus]

There are bulldozers
over our words when we meet, and in their blatant
        and their silent din
inside our chilly trailer where there's no restroom
        and no fountain
to wet our throats, as Temp IV gets razed,
        we speak at an early hour
with the wash of sleep's soundless sea about.
        Out on our words we raft
toward each other's nameless strangers
        evoked in the clouds
around the chalk's clear lines. Erasure
        of the warm-up exercise
for consistency of person spins off a vague nebula.
        Eloise reads aloud
her persuasive essay appealing to the authority
        of hungry children
whose needs "got tabled unfed with the free
        school lunch cancellation."
And Tim, wide awake as a fellow critic, quotes verbatim
        the text's limitation
of such expertise based on personal testimony.
        He talks at blackboard ghosts
of unabsorbed white words. Then once more
        we look for the significance
of structure inside a temporary structure, and we
        study form and function,
how Talese's "irresistible seductress" is his sibilant
        sound. And Helga snickers,
"Growing minds should have equal rights
        to their physicality
as our words do," putting on her coat to find a restroom.

Somehow we're all struggling human heaters in the icy caress
        of straight-backed chairs
even straight-spined backs recoil from,
        and something gets crushed
by too much clarity, like whiting-out the margins
        of our lives
where we probably do most of our living.

We wake each day
without terms, our thoughts like protostars
    needing their clouds
to fuse. So for next time don't read the text
    for at least 24 hours
before you write because there's something to be said
    for an emptying of mind
and its thirst for the spirit of the fountain.

With your freewrites fluttering in the early wind
    of dream's undertow,
take a look down those endless corridors
    of letters to come
to at least touch what it is, you somehow
    already know.

Nostalgic

You may have heard her thrumming before you left,
this is for the one well dressed and shoed, clutching
     her breakaway beads like a bandoleer, as she clips
and clobbers any toddler in her Napoleonic course
     toward the city of plastic-snap blocks in the Sun-
shine Day Care Center, a muted sparkle in her eyes —
     this is for Adrianne.

And this is for the one she knocks over, the one
way in the cardboard corner you probably couldn't see
     get knocked over by the hard block of time till
someone comes, and no one comes to pick him up,
     and no one can see he's been knocked over —
     this is for her brother Jonathan.

You may have glimpsed him through the crack
in the doorway in your hallway on your way,
     this is for the one marooned in a walker
for an hour and a half, wedged between a wall,
     where family faces hang, and china breakfront,
not crying, not kicking, and for his sister
     wedged within the mechanical repetition
of her question — What color is water? —
     all morning — What color is water? — unanswered,
so she is unfreed to ask any other of Maria,
     the non-English-speaking housekeeper, hired
at the birth of the baby to free their mother
     to enjoy her children more when she bought
the china store, when Maria had left her own
     children in Haiti to raise money to raise them
free over here, who has been secretly next door
     for an hour and a half taking up the laundry,
and when she takes up the baby, it's to bathe
     and balm his bottom soft and clean as the sheets —
     this is for Daniel and Heidi.

Sometimes you brood in the afternoon, missing her
at the ditto machine, bound by paper reams, this is for
     the one who wakes at night to wander through drafty
rooms and drafty arms of tired dreamers, dragging
     a wet sheet behind her, and hungry for something
sweet, who finally falls asleep on the wood floor
     and wakes again with her arms all bound —
     this is for Mary.

You may have called her many times during coffee
breaks at Stony Brook U. where you are respected
         as a marine biologist with a research grant
on the line if you didn't return this term,
         this is for the one moored to your key
that imprints its cord as a faint red trace
         around her neck — yes, she locked the door,
had snack, loves you — with her box of munchkins,
         VCR remote, 37 channel cable TV box in hand,
this is for the one you need hardly call
         a drain on your time, space, self-actualization —
         this is for Lorraine.

You may be there with him most everyday,
this is for the one listening for the faintly
         remembered in the voice that goes drifting
further and further away toward its distant
         kingdom, the one who hears an unraveling
in the thrum woven of castles and kisses
         as the voice unstitches, deep-pitches
to sleep, and *Rumplestiltskin* drops in
         on the one who always seems to have a cold,
playpenned by a goal-fired dragon burning-up
         all the energy of that gold-spinning voice —
         this is for Steven.

She may be the one who gets the most
blown kisses, this is for the one who doesn't
         question, just slips into her bumpy-ride belt
at kindergarten's end and is off to her new mountain
         home, her third sleepaway summer in the wide-open
spaces and thin air, the seasons her teeter-
         totter, the one too young to question her trinket's
place on the cobwebbed pasteboard, too young to question
         her position in the relay race of waifs and strays
of double-incomed, inflation/liberation-bound
         households, too young to question the hot-potato
relinquishments of surrogate parents, no more than
         children, who leave her to wait in a foxhole
during color war —
         this is for Jennifer.

You may have packed up his favorite lunch
and driven him off with such a long last look,
         he'll remember nostalgia's hurt, not as the longing

for what was, nor for what never was, but as the longing
          for what almost came so close to being, you see,
this is for the rich one, a hundred quarters heavy
          in his pocket, alone in a kid-packed arcade,
holding in his breath before the Pac Man game
          that flashes signals like x-rays to what his
digitally scored morning-to-afternoon, wordlessly
          pinned to finger-tamping, lightning-ball flippered,
Tilt! Tilt! movements skeletally reveal,
          this is for the one who curses and kicks the machine
and then, drops another quarter into the slot —
          this is for Matthew.

          You may be personally related as a distant kin,
you may even call him godchild, this is for the one
          who has eaten his way through his father's
double-fast, once-a-week burgers'n fries,
          his father's lover's rich pastries, his mother's
sodden stews, his mother's lover's tossed salads'n
          beans, the sitter's frozen-centered TV dinners,
psycho-therapeutic overweight camp for a full summer
          of biting gnats, consciousness-raising, encounter
style Overeaters Anonymous for a full year of biting
          legal terms for his maintenance and support, and
when no one's home, he comes to you straight
          from summer camp to dab his body cushion
with your little tube of After-Bite, this is for
          the one who asks you — Whatcha got for snack? —
this is for Jeffrey.

          You may have seen his reflector flash
and swerved away as you turned into your
          driveway quick, late some cold November night,
this is for the one who gets by in your neighborhood,
          this is for the one who cranks his moonlit metal
gears like time gone heavy as the night all alone,
          10 pm, on his 10-speed bike, racing for the covenant
through the burn of the wind, till someone comes home,
          this is for the one in high gear, and the faster
his pedals, the fiercer the wind, the slower
          this thrashing out a darkness alone, this is for
the rainchilled one on an endless coastline
          of shagged leaves, and tree claws reach down for
a small boy of seven, this is for the one
          you may have rolled over in your cozy bed to wonder,
Whose child is this? —
          this is for the one whose name you never know.

Mother, how could you know your echo
your shout up the block would stir
on your way from Evergreen Avenue, all made up,
to the J & V Construction Co.'s books
you kept with dedication like one of the loyal myths
of the Great Depression, the devastating divorce
your mother kept, the need for distance inherent
in the excruciating closeness of the czar's pogrom
her mother kept, and so it echoes for the one
this is for, who is still curled up on the stoop
in the timeless courtyard, thrumming against its
cement blocks for you to come home, come home,
for when you did, it was in the decline of the day,
in the decline of your strength, this is for the one
passed from neighbor to neighbor, with a tennis ball
soaked in puddles and battered to a lone baldness
of itself against the cement blocks, looking
through the audience block when she dramatized Gretel
following a trail of crumbs, for the familiar
hazel eyes, almost golden in that certain light,
this is for the one who nostalgically dedicates
her longings nurtured in the longings
of those hazel eyes hazy with elsewhere
when you were home for a long stretch of a year,
out of work and worn with the guilt of goldbricking
with the one who was time hanging on your hands —
this is for Gayl.

And as the growing seasons know no genuine divisions
from that primeval, rotting mulch when the 1st person rose
as a mythic *I*, she may have ripened away from you
to get toward you, who found those tissues soaked
with his blood, and a neighbor calling you
to come to him in the emergency room
when you came home tired and justified
from teaching others' children to write poems,
this is for the one scarred by the hard iron bar
supporting your flower box that he walked into
when you were out, and opened his six-year-old head
to the bone, the one you had the looking-back-good-luck
to hold close a long time, guiltlessly, because
it was the economy that crunched you off
the work force (for you'd have lacked the courage
to forfeit your licensed identity when the Board's
maternity leave was through), this is for the one
munching in the middle of the stairs, waiting
for this poem to be done, before the next one —
this is for Paul.

[87]

You may remember him from somewhere you were
entwined together, this is for the one whose whisper
        grows to balmy laughter at an open doorway home
from school, from a dim, wintry road into a lit
        kitchen, rippling with cocoa steam and a woman's
warm enthusiasm for his hoisted landscape,
        a golden monochrome he fingerpainted for her
like the solid gold egg possessed by a giant,
        pursued by a boy throughout all his adult years —
        this is for the one you may remember.

On a Parallel Rooftop: Our Mutual Clutch

To their eyes our eyes are mirrors.

We were in a vast hall of students,
   proud of our instruments, then on long
lines of amateurs, patiently waiting,

waiting on illumination. We inched up,
      invigorated by the wind and our mutual clutch
         on our crude instruments. We were patient, proud

         strangers strangely keeping each other's places,
      basically amiable, often well-intentioned
the way we could afford to be

with such a toss-away responsibility:
      "Go on, warm up inside awhile. I'll keep
         your place. Just remember the color of my coat."

         Smudgy with star chart on our skin,
      we had a knack for adaptation,
for making a wry joke or two

on the university rooftop —
      like the one about the poetry student
         convinced he had been saved by a poem

         in Chinese hanging in Hung Fat in Chinatown
      that was a modified version of the Heimlich
maneuver. We were waiting our turn

at the big scope with our children clutched
      by our own wonderment * * * * *
         From the magnetism of the name and address

         in *Star Hits Magazine,* Paul began exchanging
      letters with a Russian boy, Yuri Papov,
also news and pictures of Culture Club,

and simple promises any but antipodal pen pals
      could keep, like looking at Halley's comet the same
         moment on a parallel rooftop under a parallel of night

to be able to see for themselves if its tail
always pointed toward the left or right
when Paul's night was Yuri's day

and Yuri's night was Paul's day;
or Yuri's visiting our house at graduation
"to hear CC together . . . People used to think

it was just ok for 'stars' to be eccentric,
but all that's changing," Yuri wrote.
"I have great friends." They vowed

they'd aim their instruments of wonder
at each other. Then Yuri's letters stopped.
We were waiting on parallel lines somehow,

they saying their matters, our antimatters
saying we, each with expensive flybys.
Yuri's uncle died in Afghanistan.

Paul's cousin died in Vietnam.
We were waiting on parallel lines,
women laying their hands on sons' shoulders

nudging them toward the big scope.
That Giotto's painted promise,
that flary-tailed brilliance

just seemed a fuzzy tennis ball
was irrelevant because we got familiar
with waiting to see something much farther away.

Afternoon at West Point

Military history is growing intellectually fashionable again.
The number of specialists in the field is growing at perhaps
three times the rate of a decade ago, and there is evidence
of sharp undergraduate interest in the subject. **NY Times**

Such a Sunday excursion would have been unthinkable
when I was college-bound, ending each day in revelation —
now the bloodied heads of pacifists at Columbia,
marching in waves of Phil Ochs' "I ain't a'marching anymore"
were oxidized like vague faces in an iconic old yearbook.

Yet here we were with our best friends overlooking
the misty-eyed Hudson, cliff tops and pointed certitudes
obliterated, and our kids bickering over who shoots
the pictures, as we posed with a cannon of the War of 1812.
It was a slower oxidation of all our canons over the years

that made us, I supposed, take and label shots of ourselves.
Actually, I never marched for peace. Maybe we only memorized
many faces of vagueness, like those of *Duty, Honor, Country,*
a flickering main theme projected for visitors on a screen
in a blind-bound room, where history is a tale told

by a retired officer with polished buttons and tone
and colorful canons for visual aid — "History is the best way
to focus on the operational level of war. Students are given
situations in Europe, the Middle East, Central America, etc,
and told that the President has decided to send them in.

"They make plans for assembling, transporting, and sustaining
American forces. We are interested in the reasoning process
that these guys will go through in the real world."
He gladly guided us through the garden where the budding
blond assassins of the Profession of Arms (steeped

in the curriculum of War and Military History, Military
Doctrine, The National Security Process, Strategy, War
and Operational Planning, Contingency Planning and Applications
of Power, etc) intermingled with the spirits of fragrant trees,
each nailed with a different graduating class, '39, '59, '89,

etc, of honored US prime. Behind each nail was a rusty hilum
unhealed of its ideals and cannons each enlightened class
kept vaguely issuing in its living fragrance. The sap
bead of the lush maple class of 1885, under the full-summer,
establishment-green leaves, was too high for kids to read.

As specialist in the field, he gladly wound our way
through the cultivated rows of cannons and budding
students of cannons' canons to honor the Mexican War,
the War of 1812, the Civil War, the Spanish-American War,
the War of etc, till cannon, like most cultural chameleons,

assumed hi-tech form. The kids' favorite was the Revolution
with its carefully executed scrollwork, such beauty
evoked a "Holy Shit!" from our friends' 8-year-old,
and a dirty look of "why can't you control your child?"
from our guide whose heart was clearly in his garden,

and a reflexive kick from her older sister, which evoked
a knee-jerk promise from their mom to stuff them both
inside cannons. While she was disclaiming them
and her own profession of arms, a demonstrator
was declaiming: "Do you know what this place is about?

"Do you know what's under the veneer of a liberal
education here? Do you know what's under the fancy
uniforms here? Do you know (pointing at me) what this
place is about? Do you know? It's about —" provoking
immediate detainment for her, and a cheer for her

from me, loud enough for my husband's arms to drop
next to me: "Show some respect. Do you know where you'd
be, Ms. Idealist Leibowitz? In an oven in Auschwitz
with all your poetry." This provoked an image of him
during the Vietnam war, sorting letters by size,

not destination, when his homebound National Guard unit
was called up to serve during the US Post Office strike.
I invoked Desdemona on her deathbed with her will
"not to pick bad from bad, but by bad mend." But, of course,
you know I mentioned the strike in the car on our scrappy way home.

On An Unseen Tree

[*We were surprised.*
James M. Barrett, deputy director
of international engineering for
A.T.&T. (The NY Times — *6/11/1987*]

In the light an unseen tree rustles
its pressed rings between my fingers
as they pass across the cables strung
along the ocean floor. The sharks come
with their inexplicable taste for what-
ever links the continents. They gnaw
bloodless holes through the main artery
for global voice. Their teeth embed
the cables and smear my fingers black,
while the Venice talks conclude, and
the tree rustles with self-pleased
congratulations and no breakthroughs on
the AIDS epidemic, nor S. African racism,
with tumbleweed imbalances in trade, pay-
ments and debt at a standstill between my
slippery fingers. The Persion Gulf dimples
like a fossil within the tree's wishful
ring. *I think the most important thing*
is there are probably no surprises,
Howard Baker crinkles in the leaves, while
lightning launches rockets in their poise
on a launching pad to anywhere unknown,
and the officials, who are huddled together
in a blockhouse to escape the storm,
startle at the starward tracks of their un-
preparation, while I recline in my snug
slippers to wonder if anyone is ever pre-
pared, while a federal advisory committee
envisions within its white columns
a new capability to track the movement of
a person, and guarantees only the suspicious
will get the national computer noose.

In one rustling fold, the endorsed national
computer fits into the biotechnology park
for Washington Heights, and the law-
enforcement officers track academic and
commercial research by the year 2000.
In two, lightning launches covert military
aid to Angolan rebels. And so the news folds
into itself like a paper fortune flower
I played as a child for a lifetime's surprise
of fame and flame tucked under little flaps,
and I toss it aside. When I touch my son
upon the shoulders, my inky fingers press
their print.

Freewheeling

Wind-blown, I wind through the momentary
shapes, the gesturing trees, the grinning
picket after picket, the spreading forth
of porch after porch, the secret moves
one boy on a skateboard makes.

The prissy sky seamstress tears open
her seams, and a cracked street sundreams —
nothing is seamless, even ease has
fine lines. In each curve of the body
is the mind's prism where the light may break

just so, and oh, such spectral reveries. . .
Freewheeling this way, this atheist can pray,
let me die with my feet on my pedals —
a shrill whistle warns the children
to leave their play and find their places

on line in an elementary schoolyard
as I pump by. Russet clouds are yanked
apart like curtains on another childhood
schoolyard, concrete beneath our book bags
in a row, and Toni was "It!" Do her

scissor step, soles apart, soles together,
over the sham leather, stamp twice,
touch the buckle with your nose, see
your eye flash Boo! hop
with one foot agog in the icy air

across the second bag — "You touched it!"
"You're out! You're out!" — to the back
of the line of giggling, would-be-"It" girls —
till a single whistle's throttling "Freeze!"
a double, "Line-up!" without being "It,"

just one of the finger-on-lips ruck
filing upstairs — "Who talked?" "She talked."
"Get out!" — to the back of the size-places
line filing upstairs, to place
our heads down on the wooden desks

and stare down the dry ink wells
with metal lids open to a bottomless

silence Mrs. Rich called order —
till we could "hear a pin drop."
Giggles could travel just so far

down that well. For the most gold stars,
one for each day we talked to no one,
I'd get the box of crayons in June.
No one every saw her drop the pin,
but each afternoon we'd be granted the right

to speak between the lines of hands in the air,
to write purple verse between the blue
parallels on a looseleaf page, to keep
our numbers in little square boxes
so even the mark of infinity was secured —

oh, to speak between the lines of hands in the air,
at the Astronomy Jamboree where once a year
we brought our sons to look at infinity,
that night, when our cross-currents aligned
around the alien astrologer who dared be our guest,

who dared declaim at the wooden podium
how our personalities are permanently fixed at birth
by the earth's magnetic field of the moment.
But beneath our analyses of his false analogies
that piled around the peeping-over-spectacles man

like accumulations of logical snow, each flake
of our arguments somewhat crushed under the pressure
to speak freely against his audacious profanity
to equate human beings with bar magnets.
Some wounded tremor stirred, then fell

with him, as he shuffled to the back of the room
with his notes rucked, and sat down
into silence. When the dome wheeled around
on its axis, we looked with a high-powered lens
for how the awesome planets aligned in the dark . . .

The wind is blowing its own whistle —
human affairs are flying around in their columns
of paper. Only fence shadows seem unperturbed
on this long-familiar route I follow
that suddenly can shape itself free to wonder

I'm going . . .

Bittersweet

It may behave
pruned on a trellis —
I wouldn't know.
I know the pale gold-
podded, crimson-hearted, erratic
embowerer, how rampantly
it weaves its own rope
around its climbing,
and holds itself down
and/or up —
who can tell
what keeps the hardy thriving
in all soils. On this bed,
this time, the acid
is all mine
as we lie entwined,
tumbling without grace,
sprawling like the vine
over the problem is
I can't lose myself,
on this blurry
bittersweet sheet,
forgive me.
You and I are iconic
on this permanent press gold
fruit bleached paler and
paler with each washing.
And you're never as handsome
as when you're unshaved,
entangled in your own
hairy weeds.
And I know
it's a whorish sin
for a wife not to ungather
her hand from her husband's,
not to be brazen and leave
through the milky ferns, shimmering
in her reach —
be back soon —
forgive me, fresh from the garden
these armfuls of bittersweet,
the Staff Tree that saves
indoors, fruited all winter,
and can weave its way
through fantasies. Truth is,
I stayed.
Forgive me.

Overlay: On the Spur

To the horses, frothy horses, breaking
into rainbow hooves, raging, leaping
capriciously therefrom the dipper,

he spreads his viridian wave wherever
he pleases. "Hell, can't wait
till I'm good

to start!" He takes one by the tail,
lets it drag him, drenching tangled sable
hairs in his fingers in the plunge

through whitecaps, churning his pigments
up from his undercoat, up for air,
sunsprayed rose madder

genuine, alizarin crimson watereyes.
Some foals squeeze out premature from his tube
to die albinos before the wind.

Uncharted hues gurgle suggestions of hide
he hardly recognizes — even his cankery coat
streaks out before him vague and charging.

"So what if my sky looks coarse,
hell, my colors not translucent enough
for horses galloping foam.

It's the wind, that restless old wind that surfs
on wind that matters — the rainbow's busted flankbone
bone be damned."

Northern Lights

[for Uncle Jack]

From the shoal of the ship's pool
where the dream rose as a mammoth wave
with the sway of your excursion, the rocking
water was a warning, "Get out of the pool, Jack!"

From the floodlit hand massaging your heart
where the needle spurted adrenal fire,
with the jolt of the paddles, the lightning
startled your wind's hues, your seasoul sound awakening anew,

From the portal the purple Indian corn crossed
where you bestowed your strings and reeded winds
with balalaika biased on your paunch, the Thanksgiving
we didn't know the song our dissonance met in music,

From the salt stick, "You should have plain, Jack!"
where your spittle hufed, "So I'll lick it off!"
with a rap to Aunt Leona's roast rump, the riding
"How can they stop me. Tell me I won't grow old?"

From the obese quadruple-egg raw onion hero
where the rotunda of your mouth opened on your dream
with that day sanctified by the cycle, the counting
"Only four eggs per month, Jack!" — that being the time of the month,

From the fjord's fluid shave to the glacier
where your vessel's horn shrilled off hunks of ice
with the bloodwave's lashback as you sprawled, salted, wetfaced, the
     will shimmering
aurora giving unreliable illumination,

From your underground electric passage to see *Da* — cause they said you're
     Hughes' spitting image —
where you fell wheezing through a breathing hole
with Aunt Leona's forced air your prompter, "They're coming, Jack, they're
     coming!" — the showgoers knelt in neon auroras — "The holding
heart can't sleep," you muttered, and rode with the sirens again,

From your cloudwhite hospital gown you creased a smirk
where adventure arose, in Alaskan caves lined in bluegreen ice breaths
with the couple you met no one else would speak to, the tundra blossoming
"U.J., what spirit in you!" and you feigned a fifth was beneath your gown,

From the snowpeaked Parkinson tremors the cleansing hug
where your arms' holding inlet overflooded into waves, "Goodby,"
with our kiss we were leaving again, Uncle Jack, was that the last, "The vanishing
Eskimo's name-soul lives forever," you said, "he marks his grave with jawbone,"

From the bed where they pronounced you dead, thrice, to the bed you still sell
where you rose with posturepedic mattresses at Mays Department Store
with 80 years, "I still chase women but I've forgotten why!" the jawboning
"An eclipse of the sun comes once in a while, but an Eclipse mattress is forever,"

From your see-through face sliding in-and-out the revolving hospital
        door to the golf course
where the instructors said, "You shouldn't play, Jack!" and you banged
        their backs
with bare skin, "It's almost always not now. Ghosts go where they will!"
        the teeing-off
got easier past the first freeze over day-broken landscape,

From the ivory crusts on your chin, the keysong you lured, the walrus
        tusks you gloated got your signature,

From you who assumed man does not live to eat alone, so we all had to
        overeat with you,

From you who declared, "Most people's hair gets lighter with age — my
        head gets lighter!"

From you who announced, "If we eat early I'll eat later, and if we eat
        later I'll still eat later and I'll die at 109 instead of 110,"

From you who couldn't recall why you did what you did yesterday, but
        the melodies from 14,000 days lyrics ago kept making their
        promises across your keyboard,

From you who watched exuberant Eskimos dancing in Kotzebue on Independence
        Day, who held the beating membrane of a walrus-liver drum, who
        digested muktuk and absorbed nitroglycerin,

From you, Uncle Jack, you free-lance tundra blossom, a wild octogenary
        forget-me-not, who's known the sea's northedge, the indomitable
        floe-break, the pristine lure of bald ice — did you hear the bells
        swell in light, did the current lead you slowly blue, did your
        haggard body haul you back as a supply-laden husky strains over
        jumbled sea ice? —
and you answer in bowstring and a vibrating wrist.

Warrior Fire

Out of an ancient savage battle cry
when the drum on the deathbed beat,
and a withered, sapped woman rose
restored in otter skin and shaman beads
on her own two feet, the smokeless pulsation
like laughter loosening a long-forgotten peace,

Out of the bilious air deep with conception
when dawn toppled the world splashing within,
and a swollen, queasy woman rose,
soothed despite an emetic drug given
under false pretense of a soother, the researcher awed
at the graph of her faith monitoring her intragastric balloon,

Out of a 2000-year-old crowd moored to marvel and misery
when bleeding footsoles left after-imagery in history
the way suffering became hieroglyphic legend, and a woman
afflicted with uterine bleeding felt the sacred sway
of warrior fire in the flaring garment hem around the legs
of Jesus, instantly healed herself, and began to pray,

Out of the steel in a small boy's hand in North Dakota
when his love levitated a 2-ton car like a spark
floating over his campfire, and his dad trapped beneath the car
was impossibly freed, the investigative team making a chart
to deconstruct the 65-pound, 9-year-old boy-matrix into small,
measurable units defying laws of pulley, lever and lark,

Out of icy thin air poised on a still precipice in Tibbet
when uncanny human generators made heat with spiritual intent,
and bare yogis wrapped in wet sheets, breathing in, breathing
out, liberated calories within the mindbody crucible most ancient,
the cells like believers dancing round their fires,
in the sheet drying contest that embraced the bitter elements,

Out of the story dragon's habitual fierce breath
when fear first encaved fire to worship reality there,
and a boy paralyzed by polio envisioned a far window, with mind
bellows rocking him toward it while strapped in his rocking chair,
till the window took the fire of the dragon out to the sun,
and Milton Erickson redirected his legs to walk into his frontier,

Out of the "unthinkable impossible" in 50 worldwide journals
when the iconoclast Bannister ran a sub-4-minute mile,
and next year 50 proselytes ran in his offlimits hot tracks,
and the tracks were as hot on illusion's voltaic pile,
when the real was irrelevant to 1/3 the women dosed in placebos,
not chemotherapy, who shed their healthy hair to faith's guile,

Out of the dazzling vitality of the AIDS-infected man
for 9 years symptom-free, the scientific fishing expedition
seeking some unidentified chemical factor in his blood,
out of the shrunken tumor of the NY culinary historian,
who saw red and resisted the doctor's knife-happy response,
out of the valley of the shadow of death, the arcane procession.

Out of the dark frame like medieval paintings we carry
migraine, we carry insomnia, hatred and heart disease,
we carry chronic pain, high blood pressure and anger,
dancers with seizures, executives with allergies,
astronauts with success, an old man with cancer, a young
man with multiple personalities, diabetic in just one of these,

Out of the eyes' opaline calm, the centering
and focusing that reframes the tyrant's storm-wind
into a blustery wail for love, or aplomb's
balance-trainer on an ocean-wide reflection,
we primitives of peace quest that way to light,
that masterful outlook within, while raised on the skin,

Out of sheer suggestion, a blister appears
when another subject is touched with the "hot iron"
pencil of the hypnotist, and we quest the way
with aerobic exercise, special diet, abdominal breathing,
we flash cars and missiles, we light candles and rockets,
we stick our skin with drugs to illumine,

Out of the endless iconic spinnings, a mindful stillness may come
when cool fire washes the body clean, when cool fire sends through
a rippling forgiveness, an overflowing of neuropeptide pools
in channeled healing, aware the earth ignites in fruit
after heavy rain, aware the *Om* is whispering the *Word* is
whispering fiery warrior made graceful within, the pain waxed tame.

Salvation: Recovery Room

And you know,
  all around, yes
    the air may be breached
      again, and it's unbelievable
how some original child
  nuzzles just under the skin
    like joy surging in morning's
    golden-rayed
myth. There is the tonnage
  like the afterbirth of desire.
    The dream omphalos mocks the fist
      fed with tears — god, is it you? —
O, the hunchback side of the heart,
  the crash unheavenward,
    and being unattended.
    All the marigolds are blue
and each one is someone capped
  in charge of you, whoever you are.
    Moaning rises and dives and rises
    and dives in the darkest loam
that is human
  all around, and you know, yes
    if you could just leap, just
    leap through that surface
that is the body that nobody owns,
  if you could just glimpse, just
    once, what alien intimate tongue
    is pummeling its way upward
through its own stagnant swampland
  with drowning sighs
    through quicksandy memory
    to illusory rockbed,
if you could just carry your tonnage
  all that way that you could touch
    where someone begins
    moaning, beside you.

The Core

of how his peened tin sail
with its two little dents, its crooked jib boom,
and her needlepointed Grecian urn
with its auric frame, its arabesque air,
might ever cohere,

each in newfound lusters
of the other, true, only on this wall, a wall
in the kitchen of the artisans,
a boy and a woman, yes, a wall set aglimmering
this morning

with that rush of how what is
so richly connective, as a uterine twining's
unmixed blood enhances what is
most individually discrete, of what he made,
of what she made,

side by side, as she centers
and spaces them over the gaping sink hole, just so,
and she thinks, so much in this art
of how you hold a place of haphazard things
depends on this

private coherence, this single
radiant strand of perspective not quite on the wall
at all, yes, is the same core of how
his scuffed steel file with its decades of worksheets
all columns and numbers,

its A-to-Z compartments of clients
and definitive receipts, and her nicked cane chest
with its decades of scrapsheets
all words and scratches, its ether-to-solid
reversible shifts

and compartment of rejection slips,
might ever glisten so mutually within the same arcane
horizon, true, only at this window,
a window in the bedroom of the holders,
a man and a woman,

yes, a window that arcs open
on the world held, this morning, with its fractured
spectrum of sorrows and confusions,
in the hush of forgiveness, of the man of the woman
as they extend

outwards in their intersection,
out of the hubristic trance that is their loneliness,
out of the mildew-settled sense that is
their years, with siftings so fine despairs are
untrackable, yet here,

yet toward this sheen of keen
acceptance of each nick in disposition, each mere
veneer of frail souls, she thinks,
outstanding in this light, yes, is one
and the same core

of how each shard after shard
of jagged selves, like a vessel's breakage with each
unloving kept in giving, given in keeping
as another sharp splinter adrift in the heart,
might ever fuse

to such a self-containment
so that some essence of each loving inheres
in every other, in that most human
sense, the teardrop of the bloodshot eye
is the clarity

of the lovedrop, of the dewdrop
on an ever-unfurling fern of approach toward an expansive
universe that holds her mother's swollen
hands within the bloodshot eye of the unearthed
beet she reaped

with her son, within the warm
leaves of laughter of lost love's echoing through
a friend's cavernous secret, within
the solace within the sharing the nightmare
the daylight couldn't

eclipse for her husband within her
developmental writing student's revisions: "The Death
of My Father" within a glinting intersection
of everyone she has ever loved, true, only
in this radiance,

a radiance in the dark atrium
of the being of a woman, yes, a radiance that enspirits
all the abstract fragments — the wife,
the mother, the loner, the Bronx-born Jew,
the atheist,

the car pooler, the poet, the feeder
of two cats — the domestic Twinkle and the wild Pickles
who won't ever come in the house — the jogger,
the pronoun peddler, the romantic nomad rueful
for permanence,

the perfectionistic retiree
of full-time anything, the long-term student
in sensitivity training, the undisciplined
listener, the in-line market carter,
the Trivial Pursuit

ballyhooer, the believer
in Vitamin C, mind-over-the-common-cold, bubble
baths and fools — with how, winking
from the open crucible of the poem, how
"they" are "she"

Datta, Dayadhvam, Damyata, "she" is
"I" and "I" am "you" and how all inconsistencies of person
might ever cohere, agleaming against the chalk
grain of "to be" in conjugation on a blackboard, struck
with this morning's rich light.